CRO

For Beginners

A Step-by-Step Guide on How to Crochet and Start Easy Crochet Projects

By Michelle Welsh

Table of Contents

INTRODUCTION

Crochet is an art form used to create textiles. It achieves this through linking interlocking loops of thread together and can be used to make drink coasters, clothing, blankets, dishcloths, plush toys, slippers, necklaces, bracelets, pillows, and pretty much anything else you can imagine—that would mean it also includes purses and even fabric diapers. If you can imagine an object being created out of yarn, then you can use crochet to make it.

When I was growing up, this skill was associated with the older generation. My parents didn't seem interested in the skills, but my grandmother was. Watching her work was always a captivating experience. She had decades of experience and could create amazing pieces in almost no time at all. However, while she was big into crochet, it was clear that the world wasn't particularly interested. Kids were enthralled by video games and the creation of the World Wide Web, together with the globalization of the internet, convinced us we were entering into the future. It was to be a world of technology, flying cars, and teleportation.

Of course, you already know that the future didn't work out that way. We don't have flying cars. However, technology and the internet *did* take over, that part is true. Social media websites have connected people together more than ever before. Only… it didn't quite bring with it that push toward what could be defined as futurism. Instead, sites like Etsy and Pinterest have caught on and really brought back the demand for craft-skills like crochet.

While sites like Twitter and Facebook focused on keeping everyone in contact with each other, Pinterest is an imageboard where people can share photos of anything they like. Large communities of crafters came together to share their artworks and projects on the site, kind of like an online portfolio. There are more than 10,000 posts about crochet on the site that range from guides for different stitch patterns, photos of projects, to tips and tricks. This site is a bit similar to Etsy, but a little narrower in its focus and is entirely devoted to sharing images rather than selling artistic merchandise.

Etsy is an online store in the same vein as Amazon. Amazon sells a huge variety of items—from electronics to even food and other necessities—basically anything you would expect to find in a typical department store like Walmart. On the other hand, Etsy is the online version of an arts and crafts show. Most stores sell projects they purchased from manufacturers. Etsy is a tool that the crafters themselves can use to sell their products, and there are tons of people selling crochet-related products. In fact, there are more than a million products on Etsy listed with crochet as a tag.

Together, these two sites, along with YouTube and specialized blogs, have helped fuel a revolution.

Thousands of people are getting into arts and crafts. This isn't surprising; one of the things that we can discover from our modern technological world is that there is a deeply rewarding value to learning hands-on skills like crocheting (other hands-on skills include gardening, woodworking, bladesmithing, knitting, painting, and more!). These skills help people feel more connected to the world around them, and there is a sense of confidence that comes with being able to use these skills for practical or artistic purposes.

My goal with this book is to teach you how to get started with crochet, so you can begin your journey down the road of hands-on creation. I believe there are tons of benefits to come from learning a skill like crochet, and that is what we'll be covering in chapter one, along with how long it typically takes people to learn how to crochet. We'll also discuss the differences between knitting and crochet because it seems the two practices are often mistaken for one another.

In chapter two, we will turn our attention toward the tools of the trade. This chapter will go over things like scissors and yarn, and it should be clear and easy to understand, regardless of how much you do or don't know about crochet. However, things like crochet hooks and hook organizers fall into the realm of specialized tools, and most people won't have encountered them prior to beginning to crochet themselves. Don't worry though—none of the tools we will look at will be confusing to you anymore by the time you finish the chapter.

With chapter three, we move into the practical section of the book. In order for crochet to work, the yarn in our projects has to stay together after we remove our tools. If it doesn't stay together, then the whole project will simply collapse into a tangle of thread. We use different stitch patterns to keep everything together, and chapter three is dedicated to this topic. Chapter four follows directly on the heels of this discussion to move into techniques for using these stitch patterns and bringing everything together. These two chapters will make up the meatiest bit of the book, but the information within will be useless to you unless you practice the techniques physically. No matter how much information you receive from a book, it will be the hands-on work that makes it special.

Chapter five is filled with different projects that are perfect for beginners. Each of these projects will come complete with instructions on how to bring them to life, along with a list of any supplies you will need. They'll range from simple to moderately complicated, so you can use them to try out the techniques from chapters three and four for the first time, as well as continue to train them and challenge yourself going forward.

Finally, the book will close with chapter six and some words about the common mistakes that beginners may encounter regularly when first getting into crocheting. These mistakes are often simple, easily avoidable, and pretty well-informed by common sense. Yet, they still seem to crop up frequently, so, hopefully with the knowledge in this final chapter, you will be wise enough to avoid them and speed up on your road toward mastering the art of crocheting.

So what are you waiting for? Flip the page and dive into your new favorite pastime!

CHAPTER ONE

WHY CROCHET?

If you're already reading this book, then I'm sure you have a few answers to the question "Why crochet?" Perhaps you've seen some crafts that you wanted to make, or you've heard that it can be incredibly relaxing. Both of these possible reasons point toward completely different benefits. The first is all about making cool things to decorate your house or give as gifts. You could even use this skill to earn money. The second benefit points toward a much more surprising discovery.

When you look into the benefits of crocheting, you don't exactly find what you would expect. Increasing your skills, making cool things—these are all clear. However, there are actually a lot of health benefits associated with crochet that can make it into something even cooler than it first appears. It isn't just that this skill lets you make cool things; rather, it will also help keep your brain healthy and relaxed. We will be looking into all the benefits, including health benefits, that crocheting are associated with.

However, this is only the start of this chapter. We'll follow through from our discussion of benefits and take a brief look at how long it takes to learn this skill. Different projects will have different skill requirements, and this results in quite a bit of variation in learning times, but we'll set ourselves a baseline to see how long it takes to achieve. Afterwards, we will also look briefly toward the act of knitting and see how these two approaches to textile projects differ from one another, along with how they overlap. By the end of this chapter, you'll have the knowledge that will help you decide if crocheting is something you want to pursue.

The Benefits of Crochet

There are tons of benefits to crocheting; so many, in fact, that this list could easily go on for the rest of this chapter. However, we want to cover a bit more than that before we move onto the tools of the trade, so what do you say we keep the list to the top ten reasons? These fall into three categories: those that benefit your mental health, those that benefit your physical health, and those that make it a convenient and appealing hobby.

Oh, and we won't even cover how you can use it to make every cool thing you could possibly imagine. That's just a given.

Crochet Helps Fight Insomnia: There has been a rise in insomnia in the last few years. We have surrounded ourselves with technology that flashes blue light into our eyes and keeps our brain scrambling all over the place, yet we wonder why we can't sleep?

Crochet doesn't help insomnia medically. If you are suffering from medical insomnia, then you should seek out medical care. However, crocheting before bed is a great way to slow your mind down and narrow your focus. There is a physical movement to it that will help you let out some of the energy you're holding on to, and it is certainly calmer than TV or social media. If you have problems sleeping, you can try crocheting for twenty minutes or so while laying in bed. You'll be out like a light in no time.

Crochet Helps Lower Stress, Fight Anxiety and Depression: Crocheting is actually a pretty meditative activity. This doesn't mean that you would just sit there and let your mind go blank. It isn't meditation in the strictest sense of the word. However, it does take a certain amount of focus, which means your mind is more in the moment. By paying attention to what you are doing with your hands and your crochet tools, you are narrowing your focus, which has many positives to it.

The first thing it will help you get your mind off of are the things that are bothering you at that moment. Often, we stress ourselves out the most by constantly worrying about the issues we are facing. While we should be aware of problems in our lives and seek solutions for them, stressing over them constantly never helps anyone. Stress raises our blood pressure and causes many medical issues over the long term.

Anxiety and depression can also be issues. They are mental illnesses, but they are mental illness with a behavioral side to it. Crocheting doesn't cure anxiety or depression, but it can ameliorate their symptoms and help you get control over it. This is why I say that it helps fight it. Battling any mental illness is all about acquiring more tools to help you maintain control. So, while crochet won't cure depression, it can help you to stay productive during it.

Depression often drains us of our ability to do anything, but focusing on crocheting can help us alleviate some of the most extreme pain that we experience. We can focus on what we are creating and prove to ourselves that we can still push through, and still even create something beautiful while we aren't feeling so good. Proving this to yourself can be a source of power in your fight against depression, and crochet can be something you do when you are upset rather than spiraling out of control.

Of course, I want to stress that those with any form of depression or clinical anxiety should always consult a mental health professional and follow their advice. Crochet is not the answer to anxiety or depression. It can help, but there are many other tools and tricks that a professional will be able to teach you and help you with.

Crochet is Affordable: It costs hardly anything at all to get into crochet. You'll need some tools, but these won't run you down that much. You'll need some yarn, which will be the bigger expense, especially as you start to work on more complicated projects. The more colors a project has, the more yarn you'll have to buy.

However, if you are just looking to get started, then you can get two or three different types of yarn, some tools, and be ready to work on your hobby for a few weeks for under $50. As the hobby grows, the costs won't get that much higher. It's really just about how much you are looking to create.

Crochet is Portable: Crochet is a lightweight hobby. You can toss your stuff in a backpack or purse and hardly feel a difference. It's extremely easy to pull out your gear while you're sitting on the bus or waiting at the doctor's office.

Other creative hobbies tend to take up much more space. Drawing is a cheap and easy hobby to get into, but painting requires a lot of gear to be lugged around. You can't practice woodworking without first dedicating an entire space to it. On the other hand, crochet can be taken on the road or a walk, and you can work on it anywhere you have light. Since you don't need any electricity, you can also enjoy it in the park while soaking up some sunshine. It makes for an extremely convenient hobby.

Crochet Strengthens Your Eye Muscles: Crochet is great at strengthening the body, even some parts you may be surprised about. The most surprising of these parts, in my opinion, is how crochet actually helps you to strengthen the muscles in your eyes, which can then help slow down the degradation of your vision.

There are multiple ways in which we can lose our eyesight. One of the ways that becomes more prevalent as we age is through atrophying of the muscles of the eye through lack of use. Our eyes benefit greatly from focusing on objects at different distances from us. For example, if you work at the computer for long periods, you should take a few breaks, taking looks at things far away from you, so you allow the muscles of your eyes to stretch out.

However, you should also be looking at things much closer to you than a computer. Crocheting helps your eye muscles work out because you need to narrow in your vision on the different pieces of yarn that you are working with. Basically, this hobby for your hands will also help your eyes.

Crochet Reduces Arthritis Pain: Again, this is a case of reducing and not fixing. Beyond how crocheting helps the fingers and the wrists, it can also help you keep movement in your fingers when you are suffering from arthritis. This one might sound silly, but it is actually one activity that is commonly used in physical therapy to help return movement and dexterity to people's hands.

One major problem with our physical health as we get older is how we don't realize how much we are letting it slip. As it becomes harder for our physical bodies to do what we want to do, we often give up the things we used to enjoy that required physical movement. We don't exercise as hard as we once did, and, eventually, we no longer exercise at all. We understand that we lose part of our physical health when we give up on activities we once loved, but this is much worse than people realize.

People think that they are giving up the physical; however, the realm of the mental is impacted as well. We know that neuroplasticity is real now. This is the process through which the brain continues to grow and change physically throughout the whole of a person's life. From the day you are born to the day you die, neuroplasticity is happening, which means that, the more often you do something, the larger the section of your brain that is controlling the movements for that activity becomes too. So, if you practice doing something with your fingers, you will strengthen your ability to do things with your fingers too, both on a muscular level of the fingers and with how your brain changes, making you more capable as a whole.

This is awesome because it means that we can always continue to improve at anything we set ourselves to do. However, it also kind of sucks because so many of us aren't aware of this process, and we allow ourselves to fall into negative behaviors or stop taking care of ourselves. When arthritis cripples a person's hands, they do less with them. In this case, the arthritis damaged them, but the lack of use also results in a loss of size in that area of the brain. Crocheting is one way you can keep that area of the brain large, which helps to stop arthritis from taking away your motor skills.

Crochet Builds Self-Esteem and Confidence: Acquiring any skill will be a major boost to your self-esteem. It is so cool to be able to do something with your hands like gardening or crochet. Each time you finish a project, you will receive a burst of positive and invigorating emotion. Being able to take raw materials and turn them into something cool is also a rewarding experience.

However, what's even more important is what happens when you start to get really good at it. Your confidence will grow alongside your skill, and it is amazing. For some people, this confidence is only located in and around the skill, but most people find that gaining confidence in one area helps them bring confidence for them to another section. So, why not build confidence by making some awesome crafts with some crochet skills?

Crochet Keeps Your Brain Strong and Reduces Risk for Alzheimer's: Did you know that crafting skills like crochet can reduce the risk of Alzheimer's disease by up to 50%? This has to do with that neuroplasticity we talked about previously. Learning skills like crochet helps us keep our brains growing and developing healthily. This strives off the death of our brain cells and the chances of it deteriorating due to this and similar illnesses.

Crochet Lets You Multitask: Crochet takes a bit of focus, but a lot of it can easily become second nature. You can do a large portion of a crochet project with a minimal amount of attention. This is awesome because it makes crochet a great activity for doing with other things. Watching TV? Go ahead and crochet. Talking with family or friends? You can definitely crochet then.

Crochet is easy to take on the go, and it can be done without taking up all your attention. This fact makes it a great hobby.

Crochet Is Great for Socializing: There are tons of people all over the world that are into crochet. You can find people in each and every town in North America. There are stores where you can meet people who have taken up this hobby, but that is just the beginning.

Art and crafts shows are awesome because they let you sell the things you've crafted. Beyond that, they are also an amazing way to meet people who are also into crochet. You can share techniques and tricks, or give each other lessons. You could even find a mentor if you are lucky.

Plus, there are thousands upon thousands of people online who follow social media groups about crochet, so it is always easy to find people who share your interests.

How Long Does It Take to Learn How to Crochet?

There is not one single answer to this question for everyone. Some people learn at a faster rate compared to others, whereas some come in with more knowledge about activities similar to crochet, and some others have more time to commit to learning it as a new hobby. So, how long it will take you to learn will depend on you.

For a baseline, it generally takes about a year to get good at crochet. Not great—learning to crochet takes much longer than that, but becoming relatively good can be achieved within this time. You'll still need to practice for a few hours every couple days, but it is a rather easy skill to learn when compared to some of the others out there.

Yet, a year is a long time. Does it really take a year to make something? Nope. It takes a year to become good. Despite that, you can still make something in your first afternoon crocheting. It may not be very good, but you can still make a simple project and improve it with the new techniques you build. Projects that only require a single piece will be easier and quicker to learn when compared to those with multiple pieces. This is actually pretty great because it makes it easy to judge where your skill level is, and you can increase difficulty as you need to easily.

Early projects will start requiring only one or two types of stitches but the amount you will need to learn increases as you continue improving your crocheting skills. Learning these are the major roadblocks in learning. Each one can be thought of as a new plateau in your skill level. Don't try to rush through learning them too quickly; it is best to practice a stitch over and over until you know how to do it by heart. When you try to learn too quickly, you will get the stitches confused with each other and possibly lose a lot of time and work having to deal with rookie mistakes.

What's the Difference between Knitting and Crochet?

Both knitting and crocheting turn yarn into works of art; however, they are not the same. Knitting is more well known than crocheting—it is done with two needles that use stitches in the form of loops. Crocheting uses only a single instrument: the crochet hook. This results in a stitch that is more like a tiny knot than a loop. Crochet stitches are larger than those in knitting, giving it a different look to the project.

Knitting is easier to learn than crochet, but that doesn't necessarily mean it is a less valuable skill. There is plenty of value in knowing how to knit, and there are even times when a project should be knit rather than crocheted. For example, if you are looking to create something that will be worn on one's chest, such as a shirt or sweater, then you will want the stitch to be much more delicate, so it will be less irritating. For this, you would turn to knitting. However, if you're making a scarf or hat—something that you want to have a bit of weight—then crocheting would be a better fit because it would be much thicker, and thus heavier.

This difference in stitches is entirely due to the different tools required to achieve each effect. Knitting stitches are achieved by moving each stitch over the other needle, then bringing it back to the first needle, then continuing on and on in that fashion. It is a methodical process and allows the stitches to be extremely uniform. Crochet uses a single hook, so the stitches are rougher and much larger because of how they are knotted up. The movements of crochet are, thus, quite different from knitting, even if they look similar to those with little skill in either.

Knitting is typically chosen for projects that will take a long time to complete, or those with many intricate details. Crochet is better for projects that can be completed in a short time and with less detail. You are likely to make mistakes along the way, which will result in crochet being a more expensive style. In addition, crochet uses more yarn, so it would have already been more expensive to begin with. There are many more patterns and projects to be found for knitting than there are for crochet, but thanks to the internet, there are still quite a few for crochet. However, even though there is plenty, the amount still pales in comparison to how many knitting projects are out there.

Choosing between knitting and crochet isn't an easy decision. So don't, because what's barring you from learning both? You can't exactly take the skills from this book into knitting, but there is a lot of crossover between these two skills, and learning both will give you that much more control over the yarn. Finish up with this book, practice a bit with crocheting, and see what you can find about knitting later.

Chapter Summary

- There are many benefits to learning crochet.

- Crochet helps you to fight insomnia, so you can fall asleep easier.

- It also helps lower your stress levels and reduce symptoms of anxiety and depression.

- It's affordable, and, once you get better at it, you can make your money back easily from it.

- It's easy to take your crochet gear with you wherever you go.

- Focusing on the different stitches is actually really good for the eyes, which is pretty neat.

- The movements in crochet can help you reduce arthritis pain in your wrists.

- Making crafts with a still-like crochet helps you build self-esteem and confidence.

- Crochet is an easy skill to use once you get the hang of it, and that's super awesome because it helps reduce your risk of Alzheimer's by up to 50%!

- You can watch TV while you crochet.

- There are many people who love to talk about crochet, making it a great way to make new friends.

- It'll probably take you about a year to get the basics of crochet down.

- Crochet uses a single crochet hook, whereas knitting uses two knitting needles.

- Knitting is easier to learn than crochet, but it can still be a powerful way to create textiles.

- Crochet is best for short and fun projects, whereas knitting is better for long-term projects.

- Rather than picking between learning crochet or learning to knit, why not learn both?

In the next chapter, you will learn all about the various tools you can use to crochet. From our crochet hooks to our yarn, and from scissors to organizers, you'll be introduced to each of the tools necessary for crocheting, so you understand and learn how to use them all.

CHAPTER TWO

ESSENTIAL TOOLS

Every type of craft uses its own tools. Woodwork has saws and sanders; metalwork has a forge and anvil; painting uses brushes and a canvas; and pottery uses a wheel and kiln. Every single art form, aside from acting and narrating (although they, too, may even use scripts and writing), has a set of tools that are unique or used exclusively in a specific way to its form. Without these tools, one could get close to learning the art form, but they will never truly be able to replicate it.

Therefore, if one wants to properly crochet, then they must learn to use the tools of crochet. However, these tools aren't that difficult to understand, and there aren't really that many of them. Crochet is a surprisingly tools-lite form of crafting. There are a few specific tools that you must have, as with anything, but only a few. The key is the crochet hook—everything else besides that is a secondary tool.

We will be highlighting the secondary tools anyway in this chapter. We'll look at our crochet hook, don't get me wrong, but we'll also look at those secondary tools that we make use of when crocheting. Once you understand the tools, you'll be able to plan out your shopping list and dive into this new, wonderful hobby.

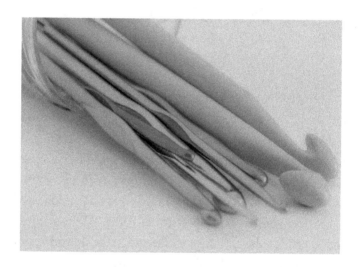

Crochet Hook

A crochet hook is a tool that allows you to make loops with your yarn. These loops lock together to form a knot, which then makes up the base crochet stitches. The crochet hook is a long tool with a straight body like a hammer, fork, or screwdriver. The end of the crochet hook is turned in a point that makes up the titular hook component. This hook forms a groove, which the yarn can catch on, and you would use it to bring the yarn back around in a loop before tying it off in a knot.

Crochet hooks come in different sizes. The shaft of the hook is designed to keep a certain size diameter. This allows the crafter to keep their loops all the same size, so the end product looks beautiful and well-made. If the loops were all different sizes, then the resulting product would seem quite poorly constructed.

The crochet hook is held typically either in a pencil or knife grip. Those using a pencil grip hold the hook like a pencil, with the hook going over the section between the thumb and the forefinger. The knife grip has the hook going under the hand in the same way you would hold a knife that you were using to cut a steak.

Crochet hooks come in different sizes. The United States has a standard size for crochet hooks and knitting needles. The smallest is 2.25 millimeters in diameter, which would be equivalent to a US #1 knitting needle of a B-1 crochet hook. #2 is 2.75 millimeters, crochet hook C-2. Sizes go up similarly, each becoming bigger and bigger, corresponding to another needle and hook. The largest has a 25-millimeter diameter. In knitting, this is equivalent to the #50 needle. In crochet, this size is called a U.

Crochet hooks are mostly uniform. I say "mostly" because this isn't always the case. The US system has created an easy and convenient way of figuring out what size you need your hooks to be, but they aren't the only authority on the matter. There are different sized hooks used in crochet that aren't available with equivalents in the American system, such as the larger hooks used in Tunisian crochet. I recommend that beginners stick with a beginner's kit containing one or two different hook sizes, but there is plenty of room to continue evolving and growing your collection as you improve, so it is always a smart idea to keep yourself open and receptive to new or foreign techniques and hooks that you can use to enrich your crochet experience and give new depth to your creations.

Yarn

Yarn is a must if you plan to crochet. You wouldn't expect to woodwork without some wood, so you shouldn't expect to crochet without some yarn. What type of yarn you choose will be entirely up to you. That decision is based solely on your preferences, along with the projects you want to create and work on.

If you are looking to create something thick, like a winter scarf, then you will want to select a yarn that is either thicker, or one that holds temperature better. If you don't know which type to pick, then you may want to do some light Googling. The main thing you need to determine when picking a yarn is what kind of fiber you plan to use. These can either come from animals or plants. There are a lot of commonly used yarns that we'll look at in this book, but I want to note that there are many, *many* more types of yarn out there than just what's in this book. If you can get your hands on a rare yarn, it can be a lot of fun to figure out how to incorporate it into your projects, so don't be afraid to branch out and experiment.

The most common yarns for crocheting are wool, cotton, and acrylic yarns. Wool yarn is quite strong, and it can survive making mistakes. If you mess something up, then you'll probably just want to unravel the yarn. The unraveled yarn can then be used again. In crocheting, we call this frogging, as in, you frogged the yarn. There isn't anything particularly special about wool yarn, and it is pretty much your most basic yarn when it comes to crochet, but it is affordable and resilient enough to make it a great choice for beginners.

Cotton yarn, on the other hand, is inelastic. That means there isn't much stretch to the fiber; therefore, it isn't as forgiving of mistakes as wool. However, the fact that it isn't as elastic is a plus for projects that require a stronger hold. If you are making a plushie, for example, then cotton would be a better pick than wool. Wool is easier to use than cotton, but it is also a bit more difficult. It is easier to work with in the summer heat compared to wool, though.

Finally, acrylic yarn is easy to find in stores, comes in tons of colors, and can be quite cheap. With that said, it is important to realize that cheap, acrylic yarn is often poorly constructed, which can make it difficult to work with. Instead, you should try spending a little more money to save yourself some hassle down the road.

We will primarily be looking at using yarn throughout this book. There is such a thing as crochet thread, which is most often made out of cotton or acrylic, but such is much thinner than yarn. Yarn's size is easier to work with than crochet thread, making it a better choice for beginners, at least in my opinion. There is nothing that says you can't start making projects with crochet thread, and, sometimes, it is a better pick for your project, especially when that project would benefit from a tighter stitch. However, if you are looking to do a tighter stitch, then knitting is probably the better choice compared to crochet. We will be sticking with yarn throughout this book, but don't be afraid to switch it up and give crochet thread a try if it interests you.

Yarn comes in different thicknesses. The measurement of a yarn's thickness is called its weight. When purchasing yarn, we would select the weight we want, which will be printed clearly on the label. Each store will use the same measurement, so it's easy for people to select the proper-sized yarn without having to worry about comparing different brands. Yarn is sized and labelled with a number between one and seven. The lower the number, the thinner the yarn. Beginners should stick to yarn in the middle of this scale. A number four yarn is a good beginner yarn, though a three or a five will also be fairly easy to work with. Beginning with four will give you an evenly weighted yarn that you can use to build up your skills. Once you are comfortable with this size, it will be easier to decide if you want larger or smaller yarn for your future projects.

Beginners are served best by sticking with a yarn with a smooth texture. The price of yarn will depend on what it is made of. If you are comparing two yarns of the same weight and material, then look for the yardage to tell which is the better deal. The yardage is how much yarn there is. Two yarns of the same material should be compared to each other to see which has the larger yardage. This will help you determine if you are paying a good amount or too much for your yarn.

The final note on yarn is color. You can use any color you see fit. Picking a color will almost always be decided by the project in question. If you are crocheting together a plush toy, then its colors will be dependent on how you want it to look—a dolphin would typically be blue, a monkey would be brown, and so on. However if you are beginning with a project simply to practice your skills, then you may want to try going with a light-colored yarn. This will make it easier to see your stitches when you are first starting out. Beginners will find that they have to devote more of their attention to their first project simply because the stitches are new to them. As you increase your skills, it will become easier to create stitches without having to look so closely at the material, meaning that darker colors won't be as much of a hassle. Although this tip can be useful, consider the colors you want for the project first and foremost.

Scissors

Scissors are one of the most useful tools you can have, and that fact goes well and far beyond crochet too. I can't count how many times I've had to use scissors in the kitchen to open up a package, or how often I've had to cut out a piece of paper for a project. Scissors are a versatile tool that everyone should have in their home already.

When it comes to crocheting, you will definitely need a good pair of scissors. However, you don't want to use just any pair of scissors. Although any pair of scissors may work, you will find that you have the best results when using sewing scissors. This is because this type of scissor is designed to cut through fabric. When it comes to cutting yarn, you will want to have a nice, clean cut with each snip. If your scissors don't cut cleanly, then chances are good that they'll pull on the yarn. This can have a detrimental effect on loosening your project, and, in extreme cases, it may even cause a structural collapse throughout the entire project. So, a clean cut is extremely important, which means using sewing scissors that won't cause damage to your project.

A Hook Organizer

You don't necessarily *need* a hook organizer. Right out the back, I am going to make that clear. This isn't a necessary tool for crochet. However, if you do invest in one, it will definitely be one of the most useful tools in your arsenal. A hook organizer is a fancy tool to use to store your hooks. Rather than keeping them in a drawer, a hook organizer lets you slot your hooks into different holding positions, so you can store them easily. Toss the hook organizer into your drawer and, when you pull it out a week later, the hooks will still be organized by size for easy selection. It's convenient as all can be.

The best hook organizers will have three features—the first is that they can fit your hooks. Most hook organizers with negative reviews on Amazon receive those reviews because they weren't the right size for the hooks they were supposed to be organizing. A good crochet hook organizer will be the right size to fit your hooks, and it will also have a secure hold, so they aren't all jumbled together and loose. It should also have a space for you to store patterns and other papers as you need for your projects. Any designs or patterns should be stored with your needles, so you can retrieve them easily and continue working. Finally, it should also have some space for your other tools. You may not want to store your larger tools in the organizer, but smaller ones like stitch markers should have a place.

The coolest thing about a hook organizer is that you don't necessarily need to go out and buy one. There are tons of patterns available, only for you to crochet your own hook organizer. This means that you can use your hooks to create a case yourself that you would carry them in. You would gain a valuable tool and some hands-on practice. That's a win-win as far as I can see.

Stitch Markers

These adorable little clips are as useful as can be. They'll only cost you a couple dollars for a case jam packed with them too, so they are among the cheapest of the gear you'll be using. These look like small little clothespins, only they don't have a needle side to them. They are most often blunt, as they clip a bit over and hang off the yarn, rather than punch through it.

When you are working on a project, there will be different points at which you'll want to mark where your stitches begin and end. This is especially true for projects that are more complicated, or when you need to pause while working on it. Simply attach a stitch marker at the appropriate place, and you can always find your stitch later easily.

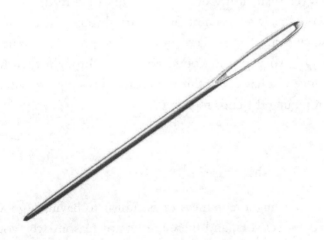

A Darning Needle

This tool is a little more specialized than the crochet hook. It is like the crochet version of a sewing needle. Crocheting isn't sewing and doesn't normally use needles, so what gives? This piece of specialized equipment is meant to be used for attaching the ends of a piece together. This comes up often in crochet, but the ratio of a crochet hook to darning needle is about 99 to 1. Although it is common, it is still only a small part of the overall experience.

As mentioned earlier, a darning needle is a lot like an oversized version of the needle you would use for sewing, using thread rather than yarn. Yarn is much bigger than nearly every other type of thread, so you would have a hard time fitting yarn through the eye of a sewing needle. The eye on a darning needle is much larger, so you can wound your yarn through it easily. Once you have your thread in place, it is simply a matter of joining the ends together.

Tape Measure

Having a tape measure is similar to having a good pair of scissors, and there are lots of reasons why you should keep one around your house beyond just crocheting. You never know when you will need a tape measure when crocheting, but it is one of those tools that always seems to be needed along the way.

A Row Counter

You could use a pen and a piece of paper to keep track of your rows, but a digital row counter is often an easier and more convenient way to keep a tally. Different projects will require a different number of rows, and you'll want to match that number with other sections of the project. To make sure you have enough, you would simply make a note every time you create a new row.

A digital row counter is worth the investment for the ease of use it offers. A good row counter will be small enough and have a clip on the back to mount it to your finger. A large button on the front will increase the tally by one each time it is pressed, and another, smaller button is used to reset the tally back down to zero. All you need to do is press the large button whenever you make a new row. At the end of a section, you may want to write down the final tally before resetting the count and moving onto the next section.

Stitch Patterns

Although we will be discussing popular stitch patterns in the next chapter, they are still also one of the tools that we can use in our crocheting adventures. A crochet pattern is a guide for creating a certain type of pattern through your stitches. They can be printed off online and stored in your hook organizer. Keeping patterns on hand in this fashion gives you a quick and easy way to reference your stitches. I highly recommend that beginners keep stitch patterns on them whenever they are working, just until they grow comfortable enough to create stitches on their own.

A Basket

Not really so much a tool for use when crocheting, but I like to recommend people get a small plastic or wicker basket to store their supplies in. The largest part of your crocheting kit will be your yarns. While it is possible to leave your yarns laying around and take them as you need, it is much easier and tidier to keep them all together, so you can switch between them easily or move them out of the way when you have company over.

A small basket with a couple handles on either side will give you plenty of support for your supplies. They don't weigh much, so your basket should never be that heavy. However, you will find that keeping your supplies together will make the process that much easier, since you never have to lose your train of thought or the position of your stitch because you had to go searching for a stitch marker or another color of yarn.

Chapter Summary

- In this chapter, we looked at the tools you need for crochet. But to say that you need these tools is a bit of an exaggeration. There is a form of crochet called finger crochet, in which you use your finger instead of a crochet hook. However, for typical crochet, the tools described within this chapter are what you can expect.

- A crochet hook is a kind of like a drum stick with a hook on the end. You use it to create hooks of yarn, then pull them through other loops to create stitches.

- Yarn is a pretty big one for crochet. You can crochet with glass and plastic if you want, but most people stick to some form of yarn, like cotton, wool, or acrylic. That wasn't a joke about the glass or plastic—read chapter five to learn more about those styles.

- Your trusty scissors. They cut things. They're scissors. Can't really over-explain scissors. Just make sure they're a good pair. It's always worth investing in scissors.

- A hook organizer can be a great way to keep your hooks sorted. As you move through a long project, you will get tired and a hook organizer can help you to keep your place.

- Stitch markers are simply colorful little clips that indicate where your stitches are for later.

- A darning needle, or tapestry needle, can be used to finish up the ends of a project.

- A tape measure is how you create properly sized pieces.

- As you work on longer projects, you may forget what row you are on. A digital row counter is an easy way to keep your place.

- If you want to make something, then you will need to know what you plan to make, at least while you're learning the basics. That means you need to find some stitch patterns, but these are usually pretty hard to read, so stick around for chapter five for some guidance on that topic.

- A basket is definitely the cutest way to store any form of fabric-working gear, so why not get one?

In the next chapter, you will learn about a whole bunch of crochet stitches. Starting with a slip knot—not a stitch, but the single most important part of crochet—you'll learn all the basic stitches, and even a couple more difficult ones. Keep an eye out for more stitches sprinkled throughout chapter five, too.

CHAPTER THREE

POPULAR CROCHET STITCHES

While many crochet designs require multiple yarns and lots of interwoven styles, this doesn't apply to beginner projects. These projects can be made with a single ball of yarn and a few stitches. The reason that a single ball of yarn works is because of the stitches used in crochet.

A stitch in crochet is simply a way of turning a straight thread of yarn into a complex pattern arrangement. I say complex, but that doesn't mean that stitches are hard to do. In fact, many stitches are actually quite easy, like the first half of the ones we will be exploring in this chapter. Complex in this sense refers to how they appear when they are finished. Crochet stitches join together to give character and definition to the yarn, creating intricate rows of repeating patterns that join together to give the project its basic appearance. A stitch alone doesn't look like much of anything, but once you line up a few of them together, it becomes gorgeous.

In this chapter, we will be looking exclusively at crochet stitch patterns. We'll start with a handful of patterns for beginners, which are the easiest of the stitches to achieve. However, don't take that to mean that these patterns are, in any way, simpler or ineffective compared to more complex ones. You make thousands upon thousands of different projects using only these beginner stitches. Beyond the beginner stitches, we'll also be looking ahead at a couple of the more advanced stitches. Don't feel intimidated if you aren't ready to tackle these stitches just yet—crochet takes time to learn, and you should practice and grow comfortable with the beginner stitches before tackling the more advanced stitches in the second half of this chapter.

The Slip Knot

This is not a stitch, technically speaking. In fact, you could argue that it belongs in the next chapter because it is more of a technique than anything else. However, if you don't know how to make a slip knot, you won't be able to make even the most basic of crochet stitches. You need a knot to begin your crochet project, and a slip knot is a good choice because the movement of making it is a perfect fit for the movements you'll make while crocheting.

Take a loop of yarn and place your index finger through it while the rest rests on your middle and ring fingers. Your two fingers offer support to the yarn, whereas your thumb is free to interact with it, and the index finger keeps it secure. Take your crochet hook in your other hand and face the hook out toward you. Slide the hook into your yarn loop, where it is held by the index finger. Lift up the crochet hook while using your index finger on that hand to hold the yarn to the hook. Rotate the crochet hook to the right until it has come around full circle. You will know this is working correctly if it twirls the yarn around the crochet hook into a rather loose hook.

Next, you want to wrap the free hanging yarn in your left hand around the yarn hanging on the hook, and then over the hook. Your yarn will look to be hugging itself, then wrapping around the hook. With the yarn now wrapped around the crochet hook, draw it back through the first loop you made back when you twisted the crochet hook in a circle. Now your slip knot has been formed. The knot on your crochet hook should be loose. If you want it to be tighter, you just need to pull at the ends of the yarn. There are both benefits and hindrances to keeping it too loose and keeping it too tight, so expect it to take a bit of practice to get it just right. You are aiming for a tight fit, but not overly so. You basically want the yarn to be hugging the hook like a friend instead of a bear.

Although most of the following stitches are abbreviated in crochet patterns, slip knots are not. It is necessary to have a knot on your crochet hook in order to be working, so it is typically assumed that you have begun with a slip knot. You may see the abbreviation "Sl," but this is for slip *stitch*, not slip *knot*.

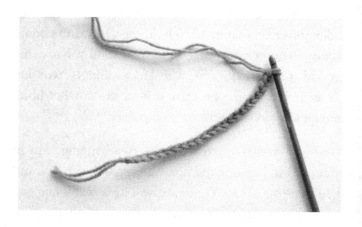

The Chain Stitch

The chain stitch is an incredibly important stitch when it comes to crochet. It is used in many different patterns for various projects. It is commonly abbreviated as **Ch** in patterns. The chain stitch is an essential part of crochet, and you won't be able to get very far without learning it. These stitches are typically used to begin a project before other stitches are added. The first chain stitch in a project is often referred to as the *foundation chain* for this reason. This doesn't mean there is only a single chain stitch in a project—there can be many, it is simply used to designate where everything started from. Chain stitches are combined with other stitches to create patterns.

A chain stitch first starts as a slip knot. Follow the guide above to form a slip knot directly on your crochet hook. Then, take the slip knot between your thumb and fingers with the knot facing you throughout. Yarn coming from your ball is worked over the index finger, then back between the index and middle to wrap over the palm, then up to the two remaining fingers. You should feel kind of like you are the gears of a machine as the yarn weaves through your fingers. This can be a bit weird, but it lets you keep a good bit of tension on the yarn, which increases the ease of the process. Make sure the hook is facing up to begin with, but it will change position in time. Keep it steady and hold it tight, but not so tight that it becomes stiff and unwieldy.

Loop your yarn over the hook like you did when making the slip knot. You can do this with your free hand if you need to. Most beginners start out by looping the yarn over their crochet hook with their left hand while they hold it in place with their right. As you get more comfortable with the technique, you will find that it is easy enough to do with your right hand alone, or whatever hand you choose to hold the crochet hook in. Some people do continue using their left hand to loop the yarn just because they have gained a good rhythm with it. Crochet, along with just about any art form, has a lot of crossover with music. There is a rhythm to the actions you take, almost like a bassline or a dance. Each person finds the beat that best fits them.

As you loop the yarn over the hook, turn the hook a little bit to the left as you do so. You'll pull the yarn through the loop, just like you did previously, but, this time, the crochet needle will be pointing about ninety degrees to the left of when the loop started. If you do this another time, then the hook would be facing the ground. Then, it would be pointing away from you. Finally, it would be pointing back up again. This pattern would then repeat until you finish. So, you would draw the yarn through the loop with the hook. Remember to keep the loop in place using the index finger of your hook hand. Pull the yarn completely through the hook, and then use your left hand to close the stitch. If you have difficulty working with the hook when it is facing to the side or down, then you can return it to its upright position. The goal is to keep the stitch as even as possible, so only turn the crochet hook the same amount for each stitch.

You will need to count the number of stitches in a chain when crocheting. This would be the first one. We wouldn't count the slip knot on the crochet hook, even though it is created in nearly the same fashion. It doesn't count as a stitch until it has gone over the hook as it rotates, and then is pulled back through and closed. You just created your first one, if you have been following along, so you would then repeat the movements to get your second, third, fourth and so on. This is your most basic of stitches and your foundation upon which to build. Make sure you practice it until you become quite comfortable with it.

The Slip Stitch

This is another of the foundational stitches that you will need to learn. Some people will argue that this is not a stitch—rather a technique—but let's not focus on the semantics. The important thing here is that the slip stitch is highly useful. It is abbreviated as **Sl st** in patterns. This stitch is used for many different purposes. It can connect pieces to each other, which makes it incredibly useful. It is one of the smallest stitches possible, meaning it also gets flagged for use a lot when it comes to adding detail to a project. It is also the go-to stitch for applying a quick and easy edge to a piece. It is called a "slip stitch" because it basically slips in between other stitches. Often, you will want to hide your slip stitch by keeping it the same color as the rest of the project, but changing the color of the yarn can be an artistic choice to make the whole thing stand out.

Once again, you would start this stitch by having a slip knot to secure the yarn to the crochet hook. You will need to have a piece of yarn that you are already working with, such as one of the chains you just finished making. Keep an active loop on your hook. Remember that an active loop does not count toward the number of stitches in a piece until it is finished. Insert the crochet hook between two stitches on the chain piece. With the hook through, use it to grab the yarn, then pull the yarn back through and out of the piece. Again, you will poke your hook between two stitches, grab your yarn, and then pull it out from between the stitches again.

To finish the slip stitch, you need to bring the new loop through the active loop. Once you pull the new loop through the one on your hook, it will disappear, and you'll find that you have a really tight slip stitch. You can continue going down along the chain if you wanted. If you started at the end of the piece, then you could just continue along the edge, moving over one stitch at a time to add a new slip stitch. At the end, you would have given the piece a border. This could also be used to connect pieces together. Rather than merely slipping the hook through one piece, you would slip it between the stitches on two pieces at the same time, then follow the same double hoop pattern you used above. This would connect the pieces together, and you can then continue along with it in the same fashion as you did the border.

Slip stitches can be used to apply details. This is called surface crochet because it is using crochet to apply details onto the surface of the piece. You would use it the same way. If you get your crochet hook through the fabric, then you can add details that way. Just poke through with the hook like you would any other project. You can add as many or as few details as you want this way. If you wanted to sign your name on a project, for example, then slip stitching the surface would be one solution.

Slip stitches may take you a couple tries to nail, but they are surprisingly easy for how extremely integral they are to crocheting. You will find slip stitches on pretty much every project you work on. It is foundational to the art of crocheting, and, now, you have everything you need to practice it on your chain stitches and get a head start on building your skills.

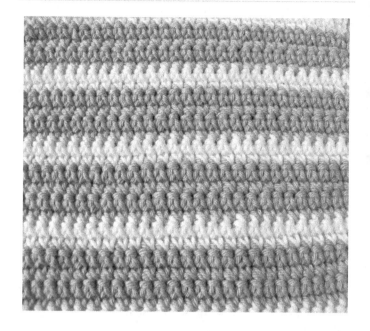

The Single Crochet

Although it doesn't have "stitch" in its title, that is exactly what this is. The single crochet is another foundational stitch that must be mastered. This is abbreviated as **Sc** in patterns. British patterns may refer to it as a double crochet, which may be abbreviated as **Dc** instead. Both of these stitches are the same. Our next stitches are the half double crochet stitch and the double crochet stitch. We will be stitching with American naming conventions, which means this is the single crochet. It is a versatile stitch that can be aligned in rows, rounds, or spirals. It can be used as edging.

Start by using the chain stitch to found the foundation chain. You'll need a foundation stitch to practice the single crochet. This technique looks a lot like slip stitching at first. Insert your crochet hook between the first chain. You can continue to go through subsequently with this stitch by moving to the second chain for the next stitch, and so forth. When you put your crochet hook through a chain like this, pull the yarn over the hook and pull it back through, you should end up with two loops. There are patterns that will tell you to ignore one of the loops, but, most often, we will be taking them both with us when we pull the hook back through the chain. So, to repeat, we are sticking our hook into the first chain, yarning over, grabbing the yarn, then pulling the hook and the yarn back out of the chain.

The result of this will be two loops on the hook. The slip stitch simply allows the second of the stitches to slip off the hook after being pulled through the main loop. This time around is a little different. We want both of these loops to be part of our stitch. This is why the British call this a double crochet because there are two loops we'll be turning into the stitch. However, this is the foundation of the single crochet in America. Let's finish it up.

Yarn over your crochet hook again, then use the hook to grab the yarn once again. Use the hook to draw the yarn through the two loops on the hook to complete the single crochet stitch. There will be one loop left on the hook, which you can then use to start on the next single crochet stitch. As with any of the designs in crochet, this takes on the most beauty and aesthetic appeal when it is repeated to create large rows of single crochet stitches.

The single crochet style can be altered to create different-looking rows. When we first push the crochet hook into the foundation chain, we would use both starting loops as part of our single crochet stitch. If we chose to use only one of them then we could create a whole different looking single crochet stitch. The front loop only single crochet stitch only hooks the front loop, as the name implies. This stitch results in larger holes between the thread, which could be used to make a piece of clothing more breathable. The back loop only method takes the opposite loop and is used to create what I think is a pretty ugly-looking stitch. However, if you start with the front loop on your first stitch, switch to the back loop on the second, then repeat the pattern, you will end up with a really awesome-looking stitch that can add some great depth to the texture of the fabric.

The Double Crochet Stitch

This is another extremely important and foundational stitch. Once you master the double crochet and the single crochet, you can then open yourself up to the half double crochet stitch, which is a real thing, even if it sounds like a parody of the naming convention. The double crochet is abbreviated as **Dc**.

Like the slip and single crochet stitches, the double crochet stitch requires a chain for you to work the stitches into. This means you'll want to grab another of your practice chains from the first stitch. Make sure you have a slip knot on your hook.

We have mostly inserted our hooks into the chain, then we yarned over and pulled the hook back out. This time around, we will yarn over the hook before we put it into the chain. Once the yarn is over the hook, we then stitch it into the chain. To create a proper-sized double crochet. we will enter the chain at the third chain. The first and second chain will come together to give us the double crochet look. After you have inserted the hook through the chain, you will then yarn over again and pull the hook and yarn back out. You will know you've done it properly if there are three loops on your crochet hook this time around. Yarn over your hook again, then pull the yarn through the first and second loop on the hook. You will now only have two loops on the hook. Yarn over the hook yet again and pull the new loop through the two remaining loops. This creates your double crochet stitch.

So again—you would yarn over your hook, then stick the hook through the third chain. Yarn over the hook again, then pull it out. Yarn over the hool again, and then pull it through two of the three loops. Yarn over again and pull it through the two remaining loops. To summarize, there are a total of four steps in which you would yarn over your hook, so the double crochet stitch is a great stitch to practice if you still don't get the hang of how to yarn over yet.

When you are doing a row of double crochet stitches rather than a single one, then it is important to note that you don't need to skip to the third chain every time. If you are creating a row, then you would start the row at the third chain. Once you have finished your double crochet stitch, you would start the second one at the fourth chain, and the third would start with the third chain, and so on. Double crochet is a super important and flexible style of stitching that can be used to achieve a lot of great effects. Don't be afraid to experiment with it to see what happens when you increase or decrease your stitches or when you increase or decrease the size of the hook you use. You can also change up how you hook the loops to create different effects the same way we did with single crochet stitches.

The Treble Crochet Stitch

Again, this particular stitch is named for the US system rather than the British system. In crochet patterns, you will find the treble crochet being listed as **Tr** or **Trc**. In patterns that spell it out, you may see it listed as the triple crochet. Both treble and triple can be used to reference this stitch, so, often, it is left up to which naming convention the author of the pattern likes best. As each stitch increases, from single to double and on to treble, there are more loops being worked. However, each of these stitches follows each other in order of height. The single crochet stitch is a rather short stitch, but the treble crochet stitch is a rather tall stitch. Because of this, the stitch is best used when you are looking for a stitch that is taller than a double. It will give you the height you want, but it will have a similar look to the double. On the other hand, two doubles or a double and a single stacked would look rather weird, and, most of the time, it has a jarring effect, whereas the rest of the crochet stitches create an uniformity effect.

To start, tie a slip knot around your hook. With this in place, you will want to yarn over hook. We would most often do this once, but for the treble crochet stitch, you will need to yarn over your hook twice. Once you have your yarn over hook the second time, then you can push the crochet hook into the next stitch. With your hook pushed through the stitch, yarn over hook again. This would be the third time you draped yarn over hook.

When you have finished the third yarn over hook, then hook the yarn and pull it back through the stitch. This should result in four loops being on your hook. When you loop the yarn back over the hook, you will then pull it through the first two loops. This will reduce the number of loops on your crochet hook down to three instead of four. We yarn over the hook again, then pull the hook and yarn through two of the loops on your hook. Once you have drawn the yarn through, then you would yarn over the hook yet again and use the hook to draw the yarn through the remaining two loops. Once this is done, your treble crochet is complete, and you will only have a single loop left on your hook.

This particular stitch is not very hard. In fact, it builds on the skills used by the single and double crochet stitches directly. The hard part of working with this stitch isn't the stitch itself, but simply making sure that you follow all the instructions. There are six different instances in which you are required to yarn over hook. If we count the original drawing of the yarn through the stitch, then there are four different points at which you must draw the yarn through a loop. Making sure you get the right number of loops or yarn to loop over your hook takes a bit of practice and patience. The movements will become easier, so long as you've been practicing the previous stitches, but the logistics of the stitch are tough to get down at first. Give yourself permission to make mistakes and try to get some serious practice in before you reach for the treble crochet stitch for your bigger, more important projects.

Basic Crochet V-Stitch

Now we're moving into more difficult territory. The V-stitch is a very attractive looking stitch and one that is fantastic for tackling large projects. It doesn't have a short-hand the same way the others do because it is actually made up of the basic stitches. The V-stitch will use a double crochet stitch, chain stitch, and another double crochet stitch. We'll look at this process in depth and cover a couple more of these more complex stitches before we move on to the next chapter.

The V-stitch begins with a foundation chain. Follow the guide early in the chapter for how to use the chain stitch to create a foundation chain. This is the first step to making your own V-stitch, though you can use any foundation chains you have left over from your practice. With the chain in place, you will want to add a double crochet stitch starting from the fourth stitch in your chain. You would work your double crochet stitch in at this particular link in the chain, so the earlier links in the chain form a double crochet of their own. By choosing to go in at the fourth link in the chain, you actually manage to create two double stitches by only following the actions for one. Skip the next link in the chain, then double crochet stitch again. This gives you half of the V-stitch, which the first double crochet stitch will function as an edge for the project.

To finish your V-stitch, all you need to do is another double crochet stitch; however, this time, go into the same link in the chain where you just did the last double crochet. When you finish the second, you then have yourself your very first V-stitch. If you wanted to continue adding V-stitches, then you would yarn over your hook and start a double crochet two links down the chain. When you finish this double crochet, you would then add another double crochet stitch in the same place. This gives you a second V-stitch. Skip two links in the chain, then add two double crochet stitches to the same link to continue adding more V-stitches to your project.

When you get to the end of the row of V-stitches, then you will add in another chain stitch. The last two stitches of the chain stitch are then given a double crochet stitch. Repeat this process on both ends of the chain stitch to have the chain serve as a matching edge for the one that began the row. An important key to crochet is the turning chain, which is used to create turns in the project. The turning chain itself will serve as the first double crochet stitch in the new row, so you can jump straight into working your double crochets into place. With a new row, your V-stitches no longer work into the chain stitch anymore; rather, they work into the V-stitches of the previous row. Instead of placing your crochet hook into the chain stitch, push it into the V of the V-stitch.

You can continue this pattern as long as you want to. It creates a really interesting design that is great for projects like blankets, hats, or sweaters.

Single Crochet Mesh Stitch

The single crochet mesh stitch is another that looks beautiful, creates a real rich sense of texture to your project, and is also within the realm of the beginner. Here, you will need to know how to crochet a chain and how to achieve a single crochet stitch. Both of these are among the easiest and most vital of the stitches you'll ever work with, so it should take you no time at all until you are ready for a more complex stitch, such as this single crochet mesh stitch.

Begin the single crochet mesh stitch by first preparing a foundational chain. If you aren't sure how large you should make your chain, then, for practice purposes, I would suggest using a dozen links on the chain before you begin adding single crochet stitches to it. This will give you enough room to really get your hands dirty with this project. Plus, it will have enough space for you to keep going and easily add additional rows. I suggest that you always try your best to achieve multiple rows of stitches when first learning. This isn't necessary, but it will greatly improve your crocheting skills compared to only practicing on a single row.

With your foundation chain made, increase a single crochet stitch into the third chain from your hook. Enter into the third link in the chain, make a single crochet stitch, and a chain stitch. You want to do this before returning to the foundation chain, at which point you would skip a link in the chain before inserting your next single crochet stitch. So, what this looks like in practice is you push your crochet hook into the chain. Doing this, you create a single crochet by hooking the yarn and pulling it through the chain and loops on the hook. This gives you a single crochet stitch. From the end of this stitch, you would quickly make a single chain link. Then, you would bring your hook back to the foundation chain, skip over a link, and insert your hook into the chain again. Here, you would make another single crochet stitch, and you would also finish it up with a chain stitch before returning to the foundational chain again. Do this until you are at the end of the row.

Now turn. This is a technique that we'll look at more in the next chapter, but it is simply turning the piece in your hands, so you can work your way back over. Most beginners think of crocheting a little bit like writing on a typewriter; you get to the end of the line, then you head back to the start. What is interesting about this is how tightly related this urge is toward the direction in which you read. If you are in the Western world, then you would be more likely to try to work from the left to the right, but those in the Eastern world are more likely to go right to left. Nevertheless, the best approach is to turn it at the end, so you are always moving the same direction.

With the project turned, we can easily start on the second row. This time, we want to single crochet into the first single crochet we come to. We will still push our hook through the single crochet, grab the yarn, and make our own single crochet stitch, then follow it with a chain stitch again. So, instead of pushing into a chain stitch, we are pushing into the single crochet stitches. We are still skipping a link in the chain each time, but this results in us just skipping the chains themselves. The row will end when we add a single crochet stitch to the last single crochet stitch on the row below it.

If you want to add more rows, then you will want to continue to follow the guide for the second row. Only the first row pushes into the chain stitches. When we are crocheting the first row, we are skipping links in the chain between every single crochet stitch. We don't worry about skipping stitches in the later rows because we only stitch into the single crochet stitches we've just set down. We are typically skipping a link in the chain because we are ignoring the chain stitches of the later rows. This is important to highlight because skipping the wrong stitches will result in an ugly and unbalanced project.

The Puff Stitch

The puff stitch is absolutely the cutest of all the stitches that I know of. It creates these raised bubbles on both sides, and they remind me of packing peanuts or bubble wrap. They can be used in rows, combined with other stitches, or just to add smaller charms to a project. Of those stitches we've looked at in this chapter, I would say it is the hardest for beginners. This is thanks to how important and difficult it is to get the tension in the stitch just right compared to the others. Considering that there are different variations of the puff stitch, it is safe to say that some are easier than others, and the beginner must be careful not to mistake an easy puff stitch for a difficult one when planning out a project.

The puff stitch is actually a variation itself. We didn't look too much at the half double crochet, but the puff stitch is a version of the half double. If you are having difficulty with the puff stitch, then you may want to consider learning the half double crochet stitch on your own. It doesn't necessarily make the puff switch easier, but if your biggest issue is with the first half of the stitch, then it should. We won't be looking at the half double crochet in this book, but I recommend you take a note of it here because it makes for a great jumping off point for later research and learning if you want to continue with crochet.

To begin the puff stitch, you must first make a chain that can be of any length, so long as it has two plus four stitches. This is a common way of describing the creation of the foundation chain in many patterns. What "two plus four" is saying is that the chain needs to be at least two stitches long for working purposes. However, it is also important that we skip over a couple of the links in the chain. We do this for various reasons, but it mostly gives us a better foundation for our project or the particular stitches we are practicing. With this puff stitch, we will skip over the first three chain stitches and, instead, begin on the fourth stitch. This is the plus four needed in the chain. The two stitches we need after are important because our puff stitch will skip a link in the chain before entering again. So, we need a minimum of two chain stitches past the initial starting four.

So, wrap your yarn around your hook, then push it into the fourth chain, moving away from your hook. Once the hook is through the chain stitch, you will yarn over it again, so you have a total of three loops on your hook. If you were making a half double crochet stitch, then you would be pulling the hook back through the stitch; however, we are making a puff stitch, so, instead, we will yarn over our hook yet again, then insert the hook back into the same chain stitch. Once you have pushed into the chain stitch a second time, yarn over again to have five loops.

This is where it will be a little tricky, if it hasn't already. At this point, you would typically have to repeat this step a few more times. This means you'll push the crochet hook through the same stitch again, yarn over, then push it through the stitch again. The determining factor in getting the size right is simply how large you want the puff stitch to be. I can give you an answer that you may like. Some puff stitches only have five loops, whereas others may have more than ten. What I recommend here is that you spend some time practicing puff stitches of different sizes to get a feel for how they are done and what they look like. Doing so will help you get an understanding of how many loops you'd want a puff stitch to be for that particular project you are working on.

Keep in mind that, if you are making a pattern out of multiple puff stitches, then you will most likely want to keep them the same size for both uniformity and simplicity's sake. This is especially true for beginners. However, I don't want to give you the impression that, just because you start with uniformity that it means you must continue that way. Those who are extremely skilled at crochet can and do play with puff sizes, along with many other techniques and experiments that I wouldn't recommend for just any beginner. With that said, a practice project that could really help you level up your skills is to make a pattern out of alternating-sized puff stitches that maintains its integrity and beauty.

Once you have enough loops on your hook, yarn over, then pull the yarn through all the loops. That's right—every single one. Most of the time, we find ourselves pulling through some of those we have lined up, but the puff stitch is deeply satisfying. There is just something exhilarating about pulling through about ten or eleven loops at the same time. However, that satisfaction does not mean it's easy. If you don't have the tension of the technique mastered yet, then this step can actually be pretty tough to pull off. Each loop you pass through will get smaller than the last. If you are having difficulty getting the hook through, then it is natural to want to wiggle it, but this can ruin the tension by snagging the loops and causing them to pull.

On the other hand, if you can get the yarn through each of the loops on your hook, then you have finished the puff stitch. If you just leave the puff stitch as is, then it won't stick around for very long. You need to secure the puff stitch, and this is best done by making a chain stitch at this step. This stitch will tie off the puff stitch, so it stays puffy. It also makes it possible to work on another row, since, now, you have a chain stitch to hook your puff stitches into rather than trying to hook a puff into a puff, which would just be trouble. When you are working on a row of puff stitches, don't forget to skip a chain between each puff; three chain stitches work for a turning chain at the end of the row, and you can start the second row using the closest chain stitch you created by securing the puff stitches.

Chapter Summary

- Every crochet project begins with a slip knot. This is a very simple technique, though not even a stitch at all. You would start every project with one, so it's still worth learning right out the gate.

- The chain stitch is the foundation of crochet, so much so that the first chain you make in a project is called the foundational chain.

- The chain stitch is used to create a chain of stitches. It sounds a little weird when it's said out loud, but it's true. If you make three chain stitches, then you have a chain of three.

- Pretty much every project will begin with a chain stitch.

- The slip stitch is useful, in that it is most often used for attaching two pieces together. For example, if you plan to crochet a circle, then you must connect the end of a row with the beginning. We would use a slip stitch to attach these two ends together.

- The single crochet is your basic stitch—as standard as it can get. That isn't an insult, of course. This stitch is a foundational stone for learning, and it will be used endlessly before the end of this book (trust me!).

- The double crochet stitch is like the single stitch, but it's bigger. It's a pretty neat stitch, and it can create some cool effects in the pieces we explore in chapter five.

- The treble crochet stitch is relatively big. This means that it is extremely tall, so it creates a large row.

- The basic crochet V-stitch combines elements of the foundational stitches to create a really cool effect. It is a rather uncommon stitch, but a fun one nonetheless if you want to impress your friends.

- The single crochet mesh stitch is another that isn't overly common, though it does create a really beautiful, mesh-like texture that is great for pillows.

- The puff stitch is one of the hardest kinds of stitches that we cover in this book, if not the hardest. It is an extremely yarn-heavy stitch that creates a puff appearance, almost like packing peanuts.

In the next chapter, you will learn how to crochet circles, create a turning chain, and change the color of your thread when you change rows. We'll also take a brief look at the many different styles of crochet that you could choose to learn after finishing this book. The chapter then closes out with a glossary of the abbreviations you'll find in US crochet patterns.

incredibly useful in crochet, so you should
create them early.

Another technique that you
how to change your colors. W
talk about colors in this b
incredibly uniform so far
beginners because
distraction right n
get these stitche
making beau
use two o

considered techniques, and which we
chapter before we continue on to discuss some potential
projects for beginners.

One of the elements we will be discussing more in
this chapter is turning chains. These are simply chain
stitches, but they are still integral to crochet. You
wouldn't be able to work on a second row of stitches if
you didn't understand how to make a turning chain.
Another technique we'll discuss in this chapter is how to
crochet a circle. We have been looking at squares and
rectangles throughout the book so far, but circles are

learn how to

should understand is
haven't even begun to
ook—everything has been
Learning this skill is great for
lor may appear as merely a
w at this stage. However, once you
s down, you will naturally want to start
ful and colorful designs, even if they only
three colors.

he second half of this chapter will get a little
irder compared to the rest of the book so far. We
won't have enough space to really dive deep into every
crochet technique there is, especially those that start to
get away from the realm of the beginner. However, we
will still quickly look at these techniques, so you can see
if any of them interest you and if you wish to pursue it
later once you have gained some experience. Consider
this section of the book to be pointing toward the next
topics and projects you should Google to continue your
crochet journey.

Finally, we will close out with a look at the terms
and abbreviations that are commonly used in crochet.
This part will be a bit of a boring read, but it is still
incredibly important. Most crochet patterns use
abbreviations, as we saw with the stitches in the previous
chapter. They also have lots of terms that are unique to

crochet. Keep this glossary handy and refer to it whenever you get stuck on a term or abbreviation in a pattern.

The Turning Chain

If you paid attention to the last chapter, then you'll probably have noticed how many of your stitches began with a chain. This is because the chain is the most important part of the crochet project—you can't start a project without first creating a foundation chain for your stitches to build off of. However, when you get to the end of a row, and you want to start the next row, then you must make use of a turning chain. It is made when you reach the end of the row and then want to progress onto the next row. How long it takes you to transition between rows—in other words, how many stitches you need in the chain—will be determined by how tall your stitches are.

When you finish a piece, you would turn it over. We spoke about this in the last chapter briefly. This allows us to begin the new row where the last row ended. When you come to the end of the row you stitch together a turning chain based on the height of your stitches. This will then help you to space your following stitches properly. The typical turning chain replaces the first stitch in a row. Single crochet stitches would end with a single chain stitch, and work would continue from the first stitch. However, any of the taller stitches would see a number of chain stitches, depending on the size, and these are then counted as that row's first stitch, so you begin from the second one in.

Just how many stitches you need for a turning chain depends on what you are doing as it helps with getting the height spacing right. As mentioned, a single crochet stitch one needs one single chain stitch, and this stitch doesn't count toward the new row. A double crochet stitch gets three stitches, and you would skip the first stitch in the new row. You may have expected the double stitch to only be two chain stitches tall, but that is actually the size of a half double crochet stitch. A treble crochet stitch uses four chain stitches and skips the first stitch on the new row.

Beginners will need to master the turning chain technique if they want to work on different rows, thus the reason it is one of the most fundamental elements we've looked at so far. The chain stitch may be the easiest stitch, but that doesn't make it any less valuable. Turning chains show up constantly in crochet, and there are styles of crochet that do really interesting things with turning chains, sometimes even making them extra long or thick to achieve different effects. As you practice more with your skills, you can play around with changing the length of your turning chain to change the style of stitches in your project. This can be used to create cool patterns and effects, so don't be scared to play around.

There is a crochet technique called bruges lace that uses turning chains to create a truly beautiful lace-looking effect. So, while your turning chains will most often be functional, don't be afraid to try adding them as decoration. They can really bring out a project when done correctly.

Crocheting Circles

Circles take a bit more work than most people assume at first. It seems pretty simple to do, but you'd be surprised. Using a chain stitch, if you try to make a circle, then, each time you increase the size of the circle, you would actually be making it slightly off from the proper shape; instead, you would have a spiral. It would be circular and even look pretty cool, but it isn't a circle.

To get a circle, you need to use chain stitches, single crochet stitches, and slip stitches to do the trick. You would use the chain stitches to create the rounds and the slip stitches help keep everything together. When you are crocheting in a circle pattern, then you wouldn't use rows; you would use rounds. You can start with the smallest round and work outwards, or you can start from the largest and move inwards. We'll use these stitches together to create circles of our own.

Start by first getting your slip knot onto your hook and then creating a chain of two stitches. This will be the center of our circle. Make six single crochet stitches in the second link in the chain. Use a slip stitch to attach the ends of the round together to create the core. We're using six single stitches because we are using single crochet; we could use up to ten stitches this way for the core. If you wanted to do this with double crochet, then you would start with ten stitches and use up to fourteen.

Create a chain of one to serve as the turning chain. Normally, with single crochet, you wouldn't count the turning chain; however, this time around, we are making a circle, so we do count it. We then single crochet into the same stitch we created the base in. This results in two stitches in this first stitch. Going forward, we will stitch using two stitches in each stitch, but they'll be two single stitches. Don't skip any stitches, and you should have a total of twelve stitches in this round. Slip stitch the ends together again close to round.

The third round will actually be a little more complicated. You would start by creating a chain stitch, which counts as the first in the third round. Last time, we put another stitch into this round; however, this time around, we want it to look a little differently. We would leave the chain as the only thing we add to that stitch. In the next stitch, we would add two single crochet stitches. Now we will alternate our stitches. The next stitch receives one single crochet stitch, whereas the one after receives two. The one following gets one, and the one after gets two. This continues until the end, when you would have eighteen stitches this round. The first round had six stitches, the second was double this with twelve, and this round has eighteen stitches. Can you guess how many stitches the next round will get after you slip stitch this one together?

Chain stitches for the turn and count this as the first in the fourth round. Add one single crochet stitch to the next, then add two to the following. Now we'll be switching up the pattern a bit again because we are in a larger round. We will add one single crochet stitch to the next, then do another single stitch in the one after. We'll follow this by adding two single crochet stitches in the third stitch. Then, follow with a single stitch, a single stitch, and a double. This repeats until you get to the end to slip them around. You should have 24 stitches this round.

You can continue adding to the circle in this manner. Round five would have a single stitch, a single stitch, a single stitch, and a double stitch as your repeating pattern. Every round adds one more single stitch before it gets to the double, and the amount of stitches in the repetition is equal to the round you are in—in round two, you just did two single crochet stitches in each stitch. In round three, you did a single crochet in the first stitch and two single crochet stitches in the second. In the fourth round, you did a one, one, two pattern. So, following this, the sixth round would be one, one, one, one, two. The seventh round would be one, one, one, one, one, two. Simply continue like this, as you add to the circle.

The circle can be finished at the end of any round after you slip stitch. If you are looking to have a better-looking circle, then try using some slip stitching to give the border a nice, defined, and beautiful edge. Already, you could use this circle as a drink coaster if you wanted to.

Changing Colors

Colors! They're amazing, and there are so many of them. They can be bright or dark, vibrant or subtle, but they are all amazing and everybody has a favorite. When you first get into crochet, you will most likely be working with a single color. This is due to how you would just need one color to start practicing. The stitches are much more important to get down; who cares about changing colors when you're just practicing your first ever stitches.

However, the more you crochet, the better at it you will become, and this will make using more colors more tempting. After all, things can get pretty boring after a while when all your crochet work turns out the same color. Who doesn't like a bit of color in their hat, sweater, blanket, or even drink coasters? Learning to use different colors in the same project is one of the most enjoyable techniques you can master in crochet because it really gives you a ton of control over the style and vibe of your creations.

When you are working with colors in a project, you may see them listed as color A, color B, color C, and so on. Some patterns have colors that you are supposed to follow, but most will give you a pattern and allow you to figure out the logistics of how you want it to look color-wise. Therefore, this naming convention should be read as the first color, second color, third color, and so on. If you choose red to be your color A, then, next time, you need color A, you will know to read for your *red*. Likewise, this concept will stay the same for the others.

Take your color A yarn and create a row or two using single crochet. While all you really need is one row, you will find that it is easier to change colors when you have more rows. It's just easier to keep a hand on everything then. We don't switch colors when we finish a row, however. You may think that doing so makes the most sense, but we actually change colors just *before* the end of the row. That way, we can finish a row in one color, and the entirety of the following row is in the new color. Bring your row down to the last single crochet stitch.

Instead of finishing the stitch, you actually want to hook a loop of color B with the crochet hook and pull it through the stitch. This gives you the new yarn for the new row. If you will be using color A again soon, then you can leave it as it is; however, if you aren't, then you may as well cut the yarn. Make sure you leave plenty of yarn to serve as a tail, so you don't create any issues with the tension.

Regardless of whether you decide to cut the yarn, you will need to finish bringing color B into the project. Right now, you have it hooked on your crochet hook, and you have pulled it through the last stitch of your color A row. The first step is to create a turning chain with color B, so you can get access to the next row. Once you have your turning chain, you may as well continue adding single crochet stitches to the project because that's all there is to it. You have changed colors with no hassle.

If you want to switch to a color C, then you can do it the same way that you switched to color B. Get yourself two or three colors and practice making rows of alternating colors. This will help you understand basic movements of switching colors better. Keep in mind that this isn't all there is to switching colors—this is merely the guide for beginners. If you really find that you enjoy playing with bright and colorful designs, then the next topic you should research is how to change your color in the middle of a row. It's more difficult, for sure, but it can make for some really gorgeous and striking displays on your finished projects.

Other Crochet Techniques

There's a whole bunch of other crochet techniques—so many that we can't even begin to dig into all of them within one book. In fact, we *shouldn't* dig into all of them. Some of them are definitely for those with a higher skill level than you probably have at the moment. However, I think that is a good idea to look at them all at least briefly, even if it is only to introduce the concept. I believe that, this way, you'll be better prepared to set your own learning and research the types of crochet that are the most interesting and fun-sounding to you.

The following techniques can be broken down into a few categories. Some deal with color, whereas others deal with the tools involved in the craft. We won't focus so much on the overall categories because they can have quite a bit of crossover with each other. We'll focus, instead, on the technique. Besides, there are some techniques that simply fit into a category all on their own, so what's the use in that?

Amigurumi: This is a type of Japanese crochet. This technique is used for making small stuffed animals by combining stuffing with crochet to create adorable plush figures. It is very popular online these days.

Bavarian: This is a popular albeit highly skilled kind of crochet that is used for making some absolutely beautiful projects with lots of texture in their stitches. It creates rich and lavish looking pieces.

Bead: This is a type of crochet that is often used for making jewelry. It can be done with pretty much any of the stitch styles we looked at in the previous chapter, but it has the addition of weaving beads into the project to create its exclusive and beautiful look. You can make some elaborate and gorgeous designs, especially for hanging neck pieces.

Broomstick Lace: This technique is named after the way that you would use a crochet hook through the loops over a broomstick. You can still do this technique in that manner but, typically, people in the modern age use a thick knitting needle or similarly sized object to get the same effect in a more tightly controlled environment. It creates a beautiful, lacy appearance that is hard to beat.

Bruges Lace: We talked about this one briefly in the last chapter, but it is a crochet technique through which you would use the turning chain as one of the main elements in the design of your piece beautifully.

Chainless Foundation: This is a crochet technique for projects that don't have a foundation chain. Most of the projects you make, especially when you are a beginner, will begin with a foundation chain. However, that doesn't necessarily mean you need one. The chainless foundation technique can be learned to find a new way around the foundation chain. You can use it in most patterns in place of the foundation chain, so it is a versatile technique to learn down the road.

Cro-Hooking: This is a technique that replaces the crochet hook. Instead of the traditional hook that we've been looking at, the cro-hooking technique uses a two-headed crochet hook. Normally, there is only a hook on one end of the crochet hook, but the cro-hooking technique's crochet hook has a hook on both ends.

Cro-Tatting: This is another technique that changes out the crochet hook for a different design. This time the design is longer, straighter, and with a smaller head. It is inspired by tatting and it can be a useful way of getting some intricate details into a project.

Double-Strand: This technique is pretty simple and one that beginners can have a lot of fun working with. Throughout the book, we have been discussing projects that use a single thread. The double-strand technique simply adds a second strand of yarn to the project. You would do all the same moves you did previously, but you would also work a second thread of yarn at the same time. This technique will take a bit of time to get down because it is incredibly easy to get your yarn all tangled up. The learning curve can be frustrating, but the end result is beautiful, especially if you use different colors together to create a really cool effect.

Entrelac: Entrelac may be a knitting term, but that doesn't mean you can't learn and benefit from it in crochet. Entrelac is a type of diamond pattern that creates quite a unique look. It is more common in knitting, but crochet can be used to achieve the same effect with some tweaking.

Fair Isle: This is also a term that is more commonly used in knitting rather than crocheting, though it does work perfectly well in either. This is a popular and beautiful type of colorwork that creates beautiful patterns. It is commonly seen on winter hats and scarfs because it can create amazing snowflakes easily.

Felting: This technique is best thought of as an after-care technique. To achieve a felting look, you need to first have a crocheted item. You would wash the item in a particular way that changes its look. It can be a really cool technique that completely changes the way your project feels.

Filet: Filet is another technique for creating a lacy appearance from your crochet work. The technique is quite simple. Most often, when you get a crochet pattern, there are words to follow with instructions on what to do. Filet crochet is just a graph with a bunch of holes through it. Use filet crochet techniques to make use of a pattern and create beautiful, old-timey-feeling items.

Finger: Finger crocheting is the easiest of the techniques to understand, but also one of the hardest to execute. In this technique, you would simply toss out the crochet hook and use your finger to manipulate the strings. Wrap around your finger and pull it like you would with a hook. This technique is one that people tend to pick up in time because it can be much easier to just use finger crochet techniques to apply a quick patch to something and minor fixes that you don't feel like pulling out all your gear for.

Freeform: This is a fun technique because it is basically an invitation to toss out all the rules. It isn't so much a technique as it is an approach to crocheting. Why bother keeping track of all the different techniques and rules there are when you could just grab some yarn and crochet up whatever you felt like? If that sounds like fun, then I invite you to give freeform crocheting a try.

Glass: This is a shocking type of crochet that impresses me beyond words. The people that use this technique crochet with glass. That's right—instead of using yarn for their projects they use glass. There are several techniques for crocheting with glass, and each of them looks absolutely stunning. It's an incredible technique and one that I wouldn't even know where to begin with teaching. It looks incredibly dangerous, yet the projects that result from it are simply breathtaking. Definitely an expert-level technique, though.

Hairpin Lace: This lace technique actually requires you to buy a unique piece of equipment for making the lace itself. Rather than building the lace into the project itself, you first create strips of the lace, and then you use your crochet skills to attach them to the project later down the road.

Hyperbolic: This technique is similar to freeform crochet, but it does have a little more structure. In this technique, you would use exponential growth to create the designs. You would continue to grow each section of the project exponentially, and the design would then shift and change in tune.

Irish Lace: This lace technique comes straight out of the past. It is a technique for making a lacy appearance with crochet, and the moment you look at it, you will feel immediately as if you have been transported back in time because it is so tightly linked to the historical past that it feels beyond vintage and almost like it should be in a museum.

Join-As-You-Go: Our main way of joining pieces as beginners is to use slip stitches to connect them together. This is only one of the techniques that can be used to join pieces. Another technique is this one, known as join-as-you-go or JAYGO crochet. It's great for projects with a patchwork feeling, like quilts.

Lovers' Knot: The last of our lace techniques, this one is a rather simply looking lacy addition that offers a surprising amount of customization. With so many lace patterns, you are kind of stuck with what you have, so to speak. However, with the lovers' knot, you can very easily change the height of the stitch to alter the feel of the lace. Of all the lace techniques, this is the one that I would recommend learning first just for its versatility alone.

Overlay: Mandalas are one of the favorite color styles for modern crochet artwork. They stretch back several decades too, which gives them more of a timeless feel than the modern patterns we've become accustomed to. They're made from repetitive shapes and designs of different colors that you would combine for interesting patterns. By far the best technique for making mandalas is the overlay technique because it uses a combination of both color and texture together to create a really beautiful look. If you are a fan of mandalas or the look of stained glass windows, then the overlay style will be of much interest to you.

Plastic Bag Yarn: This is a really cool technique that shows how people are finding cool new ways to create art and help the environment. There are tons of plastic bags all over the place. So many of them just end up being thrown out but if you like crocheting then you could try making plarn. Plarn stands for plastic yarn and it is the name given to the yarn that is bag out of recycled plastic bags. This technique is super cool, weird and modern and it can result in some great projects. Plarn is quite a bit different from yarn on a microscopic level and this results in a project with quite a few unique differences that yarn can't capture on its own.

Rag Rug: This is another technique like plastic bag yarn that focuses on reducing how much material we're wasting. Rather than working with plastic bags, this approach recycles your own clothing. Torn up blankets, raggy t-shirts, and anything else that doesn't fit can be cut up into strips and used as fabric in place of your yarn. You can bleach and dye the rags before use to get your desired color, but you can get a ton of really cool effects out of leaving the designs on the clothing in place, so the end project shows that it was made out of recycled materials.

Reversible: This is less of a single crochet technique and more of a style that you can learn to do. As the name implies, this type of crochet creates a project that appears both beautiful on the outside and the inside, and you can tell because it is designed to be turned inside out too. This is a particularly great technique to bring to making blankets or hats, as it is nice to be able to toss on something to stay warm without having to worry about turning it right-side-out first.

Tapestry: Okay, I may have said I have a favorite before, but I lied because tapestry crochet is my *absolute* all-time favorite. It can be incredibly time consuming and costly compared to other techniques because it uses a bunch of different colors, and it is all about how those colors interact with each other. You can use this style to add flavor to pretty much any project, but I think it looks the best when it is used to make a literal tapestry. Crochet tapestries are simply breathtaking.

Tunisian: This is another technique that uses a unique tool. Instead of your typical crochet hook, Tunisian crochet uses a hook that has a unique shape, and the hook is also quite a bit larger compared to the traditional crochet hook. This results in a slightly different look to the end project but one that has rightfully earned fame around the world.

Wire: This is a type of crochet that is used for making jewelry, primarily. It can be used to make other types of art but most often you find wire crochet combined with bead crochet to make gorgeous jewelry. This technique is named after the wire that it uses instead of yarn. It creates amazing patterns for bracelets, necklaces, and more, and it can be both a rewarding and lucrative form of crochet to master.

Working Different Loops: We talked briefly about using different loops in the last chapter, but it is one of the techniques that beginners should start learning if they want to become experts. Most often, techniques tell us which loop to grab for our stitches. However, we can change our decisions to use the front loop or back loops or alternate between them. Whichever style we pick will still have a profound impact on the final loop and feel of the project.

Crochet Abbreviations You'll Find in Patterns

Not every pattern will use the following abbreviations; in fact, you could find some that greatly mix you up if you aren't careful to check the source of your pattern. If it is British, then the naming convention is different for what constitutes a single or a double crochet. You'll also find that you are more likely to find weird abbreviations you don't know of patterns that go back past the 1980s or so. Many of the abbreviations are the same, but there are quite a few that have changed in time.

Always check the source of your patterns before you make the first stitch; that way, you will know for sure what you are supposed to be doing.

Beg: Short for beginning, this is used to refer to the start of a row. It doesn't need to be the beginning of the project—just the row.

BL: Short for back loop. This term refers to the back loop of a stitch when you are considering where you want to enter from and which loop you want to pull through. Changing the loop you pull through changes the loop of the design.

BP: This stands for back post, which means that you are working a stitch around the post. Typically, you would move through the loop rather than around it.

Ch: Short for chain, this one will often be written in the plural form of **chs**. This is a common abbreviation, and one that you will see many, many times. Usually, it will be written as **ch 2** or **ch 4** to tell you to chain together two or four stitches.

Cl: Short for cluster, this is a type of stitch that you may need to create. We haven't looked at clusters in this book, but a cluster of double stitches would be written as **4 dc cl** to tell you that it is a cluster of four double crochet stitches.

Dc: Short for double crochet, we've covered this stitch in depth in the previous chapter.

Dec: Stands for decrease, a technique that is used to shape a project. It is the reverse of **inc**.

Dtr: Short for double treble crochet, this is an extremely tall stitch that we did not cover in this book, but you should be able to tell from the name that it is a double of the treble, which is the largest stitch we have covered thus far.

FL: Short for front loop, it is the opposite of the **BL**.

FO: Short for finished object, it often comes up in online discussions about crocheting more so than it does in patterns themselves. That said, you can mistake it easily for another pattern abbreviation if you aren't aware of what it really means.

FP: Front post, the reverse of **BP**.

Hdc: This one is sometimes referred to as **Half dc**. This is short for a half double crochet, which is one of the techniques we discussed in passing but did not cover in depth throughout the book.

Inc: Short for increase, used in shaping your crochet project.

Incl: Short for include, it simply means to add a piece, stitch or whatever else the pattern calls for.

Oz: Short for ounces. You don't use this so much in the patterns themselves except for figuring out how much yarn you'll need, sometimes it is measured in ounces. It can also be measured in **G**, grams; **M**, meters; or, **YD**, yards.

PM: Short for place marker, this is a tool you use to make your place in an ongoing crochet project.

Pc: Short for popcorn, this is a type of crochet stitch that firsts with clusters. These stitches are rather rare to find in patterns.

Rep: Short for repeat. This shorthand will often be written as **Rep***, **Rep (x)** or **Rep [x]**. The first tells you how many times you are to repeat the following sequence. When you see it with a round bracket, it means that you are to repeat the step equal to the number in the bracket. Square brackets tell you to repeat a sequence of instructions.

Rev: Short for reverse, typically is used to help shorten other stitch types, such as **rev sc** or **rev dc** for reverse single crochet or reverse double crochet.

Rnd: Short for rounds and often written in the plural form of **rnds**. This abbreviation should only show up in patterns that deal with circles, as a round is simply what we call a row in a circular design.

RS: Short for right side, it is the opposite of **WS**, or the wrong side. This helps you to figure out on which side of the project you should be doing things.

Sc: Short for single crochet, the basic but extremely important stitch that you'll find yourself using all the time.

Sk: Short for skip, this simply informs you that you are to skip the next chain. This may be listed as **sk 2** when you are to skip more than one chain.

Sl st: Short for slip stitch, the stitch that is most useful for joining together pieces. Slip stitching is especially important for crocheting rounds.

Sp: Short for space, it is sometimes listed in the plural as **sps**. This tells you how many spaces to move or how many to skip before doing another stitch.

St: Short for stitch, it is often listed in the plural as **sts**. This tells you how many stitches you are to put into a piece at any given step in the pattern.

Tog: Short for together, this sometimes stands in for **dec** to mean the same thing.

Tr: Short for treble crochet, this is the largest of the crochet stitches that we covered in this book.

Tr tr: Short for triple treble crochet. This is an incredibly—even shockingly—tall stitch that most beginners will have no use for.

UFO: Short for unfinished object, this is often used more online than in patterns. It is the opposite of **FO**.

WIP: Short for work in progress, this is another term like **UFO** that simply means that a project isn't yet complete.

WS: Short for wrong side, this is the opposite of **RS**.

YO: Short for yarn over. This is the act of draping yarn over your crochet hook to make the proper stitch. While not every type of stitch requires you to yarn over, the vast majority of them do. So many stitches include steps to **YO** that it could be the single action you perform the most often when it comes to crochet.

Chapter Summary

- A turning chain is an important albeit simple technique. You would simply end a row by making a turning chain. This is a chain stitch. If you are doing single crochet stitches, then you would only need a single stitch turning chain. Double crochet stitches use three stitch turning chains. Treble crochet stitches use four stitch turning chains.

- Crocheting circles requires you to use chain stitches and slip stitches together. Create a chain several stitches long, and then use a slip stitch to connect the end to the beginning. This gives you the foundation of your circle, and the rest of the steps can be seen up above.

- Projects that work in circles don't have rows, but, rather, they use the term rounds.

- Changing colors is a technique that most beginners want to learn quickly. To change your colors at this stage, the technique we explored would change the color at the end of the row, not the middle.

- There are a whole bunch of different crochet techniques. A handful of the techniques we looked at dealt with different kinds of lace that could be made with crochet. Another handful used different materials instead of yarn, like plastic and glass, whereas there were even more that dealt with different uses for color. There is just an absolute ton of techniques.

- Crochet patterns use a bunch of different abbreviations when explaining what to do. If you don't understand what an abbreviation is, then it will be pretty hard to follow a pattern. Use the glossary at the end of this chapter and time you get stuck on a US pattern.

- Don't forget that older and British patterns will have different abbreviations, so it is always important to check when and where the pattern comes from.

In the next chapter, you will learn seven awesome crochet patterns that you can practice and try out at home. You should read this chapter no matter your eventual goals with crochet—even if you aren't interested in the individual projects, there are still some new stitches to be learned.

CHAPTER FIVE

CROCHET PROJECTS FOR BEGINNERS

Now that we have learned many of the stitches used in crochet and covered the techniques and short hand, it is time for us to start bringing these skills together to create some beautiful projects. As we're only beginners, we will be starting with the simplest project of all: the washcloth.

From there, we will move on to a more complex washcloth, which is one that looks rather stunning if I may say so myself. From washcloths, we'll move up to a patterned hand towel, a drink cozy, an infinity scarf, some leg warmers, and a pillow. These will take us from quite simple to relatively complex. Not so much as to be beyond your ability as it stands right now, but hopefully enough to make you a little uncomfortable at first. Remember—it's when you start to get uncomfortable that you are entering new territory. Despite how it may feel at first, it is these areas from which you grow the most in your skills and ability to meet the challenges of the crochet art form.

The following projects will begin with a quick introduction on why you may want to make this particular piece. Next will be a list of the gear and supplies you'll need. We'll then go through the pattern step by step to bring it all together. Choices of color will be up to you; just remember that we keep track of our colors using color A and color B as signifiers based on when they are introduced as first in the project. Although most patterns you find will use abbreviations as listed in the previous chapter, we will stick with our words for now, just so it doesn't get confusing. Once you get a sense for how these different parts come together from these projects, you will become better prepared when you encounter the abbreviations in patterns out in the world.

As an added note, I highly recommend that you read **chapter six** first before starting the following projects, as that chapter will be going over some common mistakes that first-time crocheters tend to make, and how you can avoid doing the same.

Project #1: A Simple Washcloth

While this project is exceedingly easy, it is still worth including in the book. I am a firm believer that you should get your first project done as quickly as possible. It doesn't need to be good. It should be messy, maybe even horrible. But then you get to make all of those mistakes beginners do early. Though with that said, if you read the next chapter before starting then you're going to have a much easier time.

This washcloth is simple to make and is probably even less difficult than puff stitches. Either way, you should be able to knock it out quickly. I like this project because it is a way of showing yourself that you can absolutely use this skill to make things. If you dive in trying to make a Christmas sweater or something, then you will likely be in for a long and unforgiving project, and you will probably make mistakes throughout the sweater's creation, prolonging the process even longer. It is easy to get frustrated and quit crocheting before you've even finished a project. So, start small, make this washcloth, and rack yourself up a win.

Materials

For this project, you will need the following:

- A crochet hook, size K.

- A tapestry needle.

- A cotton yarn, one color, worsted weight.

- Your trusty scissors.

Instructions

The first step in this project is to create a big chain. Just keep chaining them together. It will feel like it's going on forever, but you'll stop once you get to nineteen chain stitches. This will be the foundation of the project. You can alter the length of this chain to change the ultimate dimensions of the project, but you can also change the dimensions by altering the next step.

With your chain in place, you will then single crochet into the second chain. So, you would skip the first chain next to your hook and create a single crochet stitch in the second link of the chain. From there, you would then add a single crochet stitch into each link in the chain until you get to the end. Once you are at the end of the row, you then create a turning chain. Remember—your turning chain is just a chain stitch that you will use to mark off the end of a row and hop up to the next. For this project, we will only need a turning chain with a single stitch because we are doing single crochet.

With your new row, you will skip the first stitch from the hook; otherwise, you will single crochet into every stitch until you get to the end and turn again. You can keep going like this until the end of time and your washcloth reaches the moon, but, more likely, you'll want to get a half dozen to a dozen rows.

Once you get your washcloth to the desired size, you will then use your scissors to cut the yarn. Remember to leave yourself a decent tail to weave into the project using your tapestry needle. With that said, you don't need to leave too much. However, beginners are best off leaving a longer tail, and then cutting it shorter one if it is too long. You can always take more yarn off, but it's harder to add more yarn back to the piece once it's been cut. Not impossible, but really not worth the time and effort. Play it safe to begin with.

And there you have it—a brand new washcloth and your very first crochet project. It was as easy as could be. You could work in different colors if you wanted or try seeing what happens if you switched to double crochet. It's a practice project that remains useful afterwards. Plus, you can always gift them to friends and family. Practice project plus a thoughtful gesture sounds like a win-win scenario to me.

Project #2: A More Complex Washcloth

That last washcloth was easy. This next washcloth, on the other hand, will be a bit harder, but should still be pretty easy. Don't worry if you get frustrated while working on it—you're still beginning, and you'll be able to bang a project out a handful of times in a single afternoon in no time. The washcloth this makes is held together much tighter and the stitches have a really cool pattern because of the combination of chain stitches, single crochet stitches and double crochet stitches. This makes this project a great step up and ideal for learning how to combine stitches of different sizes together to create some awesome patterns.

Materials

For this project, you will need the following:

- A crochet hook, size I.

- A tapestry needle.

- A cotton yarn, one color, worsted weight.

- Your trusty scissors.

Instructions

Begin this pattern by first making a chain twenty six stitches long. Once you have your foundation chain, you will single crochet into the second chain from the hook, then continue across the row. Make sure to single crochet into each of the hooks until you get to the end; doing so will give you a sense of the size of this project.

At the end of the row, you will make a turning chain one stitch long, then single crochet into each of the stitches moving forward. At the end of this row, you will create another single stitch chain. The third row is going to be a little bit different. Here you are going to single crochet into single crochet into the first and second stitches. Once you have those out of the way, you will repeat the pattern of single crocheting into the first stitch, double crocheting into the next. Single crochet, then double crochet. Remember, though, that the first three stitches in this row are single crochet. Likewise, the last three stitches in the row need to be single crochet as well.

For the fourth row, you will then create another single stitch turning chain, then single crochet into the first stitch. Now that you have the first stitch of the fourth row out of the way, you can drop into a repeating pattern. The first stitch is a single crochet stitch, and the second stitch is double crochet, single crochet, then double crochet. Pause before you get to the end and make sure the last two stitches are single crochet.

You may think you know where the pattern is going next, but you'd be wrong. Instead of continuing down the path it appears to be going down, we will be creating a single stitch turning chain, then repeating what we did in row three. That's three single crochet stitches, a double crochet stitch, then single crochet and double crochet stitches alternating until there are three single stitches at the end. We will follow that with the fourth row again, two single crochet stitches, then double crochet stitches and single crochet stitches alternating until ending with two single crochet stitches.

You will be spending rows five, six, seven, eight, all the way up to row 29, going back and forth between these two stitch arrangements. Things change once you hit row 30, however. You will end row 29, then create a single stitch turning chain; for row 30, you will simply add a single crochet stitch into every stitch across. Create a single stitch turning chain at the end and repeat it with row 31. If you remember the first two rows, this will just be a reflection of that, so both sides are even.

Once you finish row 31, it is then time to grab your trusty scissors and cut the yarn, leaving enough of a tail so you don't have any issues with tension. Use your needle to weave the ends of the yarn into the project, and there you have it—a beautiful washcloth with a tight pattern consisting of alternating single and double crochet stitches.

Project #3: A Patterned Hand Towel

This is a harder project than the last two; in fact, we will be learning how to do a brand new stitch just to complete it. Bet you thought you weren't going to learn any more stitches from this book, didn't ya? Surprise!

We will use four different colors in this towel. It'll be great for drying your hands or your dishes after a delicious meal. The colors will also alternate, so we should have a main color that serves as the main material, then we will have three colors creating bars across the towel. The middle section will go back to the background color before we have a reflection of the three bars of color, like trees upon the surface of a lake. Although harder than the other projects, this one should still not be too difficult. We will create a little loop with a button, so we can hang this towel in the kitchen. If you can master this project, you will then have a new, amazing Christmas gift idea.

To master it, however, you will first need to learn the pique stitch. We'll start the instructions with this unique stitch before moving on to talk about the hand towel itself.

Materials

For this project you will need the following:

- Two balls of 50g cotton yarn in the color of your choice.

- One ball of 50g cotton yarn in a second color of your choice.

- One ball of 50g cotton yarn in a third color of your choice.

- One ball of 50g cotton yarn in a fourth color of your choice.

- A crochet hook, size H.

- A tapestry needle.

- A button with large holes.

- Your trusty scissors

Instructions

So, to begin this project, you must first learn the pique stitch. Begin by first making a chain that is about half a dozen to a dozen stitches long. Yarn over your hook and push it into the third chain. Then, yarn over your hook a second time, so you have three loops in total around your crochet hook. Yarn over a third time, catch the yarn with the hook, and draw it through two loops. This drops you down from three loops to two. Yarn over for the fourth time and push the crochet hook into the same stitch again. Draw a loop to get four loops back onto the crochet hook. Then, yarn over for a fifth time, catch the yarn, and pull it through all the hooks. Once you have passed through the fourth hoop, you will find that you have a single hoop left and your first ever pique stitch. You'll be using this going forward in this project, so give it a little practice first, and especially if you aren't comfortable with it right away.

We will be using a lot of pique stitches, so prepare yourself. However, we will first need to make our foundation chain. This part you've certainly got memorized by now. In this case, we will make our chain 32 stitches long, which will give us the width of our hand towel, and then each row we add will increase the height.

Our first row will start in the third chain with a pique stitch. That's right—it's the first stitch out the gate after the foundation chain. Sorry! Starting from the third, you will put a pique stitch into every link in the chain. At the end of the first row, you will make a single stitch turning chain, and then jump up to the second row. In the second row, you will put a single crochet stitch into every stitch. Then, at the end of the row, you are going to make a two stitch-long turning chain.

Now, here are the important rows—everything we do from now until the end of this pattern will be based on the following two rows. They are the third and fourth row of the hand towel, but we will refer to them as row A and row B for simplicity's sake. So, just to be clear, when we say "row A," we are talking about the third row. This is not the same as when we say color A. Color A and row A are not related to each other. The row refers to the pattern, whereas the color refers to the yarn.

The third row is row A, which is extremely easy. Simply put a pique stitch into every stitch, and then create a single stitch turning chain to jump up to the fourth row. The fourth row is row B, and, here, you'll put a single crochet stitch into every stitch, then create a two stitch-long turning chain at the end.

Okay, you got that? Good. Now repeat row A and row B.

Once you have repeated the pattern for a second time, it is time to switch from color A to color B. We covered how to switch colors in the last chapter, so refer to that as a guide for how to do it if you forgot or haven't practiced it enough yet to have it memorized. Once you have switched colors, you will make four rows with this: row A, row B, row A, row B. Once you have finished these four rows, switch back to color A. With color A, make two rows: row A, then row B. At the end of the second row, you will switch to color C. With color C, crochet up row A, row B, row A, row B. At the end of the fourth row, switch back to color A. With color A, you will make two rows: A and B. Then, switch to color D. With color D, you will make four rows: A and B, then A and B. Then, switch back to color A.

Congratulations—the project is roughly half finished. You have created half of the pattern. So, with your color a yarn, you will create fourteen rows. This will give you seven pairings of row A and row B. At the end of the seventh row, switch yarn to color D. Do four rows—two pairs of row A and row B. Then, switch back to color A and do row A and row B. Switch to color C and do four rows. Next, you will need another pair of row A and row B. Switch back to color A and do a single pair. Then, switch to color B and do two pairs of row A and row B. Switch back to color A and do six rows, three pairs of row A and row B. This brings you to the end of the main body of the project.

Cut your yarn with your trusty scissors and give yourself a large enough tail that you can weave it properly into the ends of the project. This isn't the end of the project, however. We still want to add a border to the towel to make it look truly of high quality, and we will also add a button and hanger, making it perfect for use in the kitchen.

To add the border use your color A yarn and start in one of the corners of the project. Use single crochet stitches along the border, turning with a single chain stitch at each of the corners. This is a rather simple border, but one that will really make the project pop. If you want to use a more creative border, then try one of the styles listed in the previous chapter. This style is pretty good, however, because you can use it to go directly into your hanging loop.

The hanging loop is just a little more difficult than the border, but not by much. Pick which side of the hand towel you want to be the top and select either the right or left corner, depending on how you want it to hang from your cabinets. Once you know the corner where you want the hook to be, then you will know where to work from. It's a good idea to pick this out before you start your border because doing so will allow you to use the same yarn to make your hanger.

To make the hanging loop, wait until your single crochet border comes back to the corner, and then create a chain made out of sixteen stitches. Slip stitch into the fifth chain to make the loop for the button, then slip stitch into each of the other chains, working back toward the towel. This means you'll want to slip stitch into the fourth stitch, then the third, second, and first. Once you reach the first stitch and finish your slip stitch, then use your trusty scissors to make a cut, leaving yourself a long tail.

Take the tail, which should be about a foot long or so, and use your hook or fingers to weave it through the second row of the towel. Once it has been brought through the second row, push it through the holes of the button and use your needle to sew it into place quickly. The ends of your tail should still be a little longer than you need, but you can weave these into the project like you would with any other project.

Now you have not only a great looking hand towel, but also one that is convenient to keep around the kitchen. A wonderful project for use in your own house that makes a wonderful gift, too.

Project #4: A Drink Cozy

This project is a lot easier than the last one, but it is still incredibly useful. It's easy to toss a drink cozy into your purse or glove box. Once you make one of these, the next time you order a hot drink, you won't need to waste cardboard by taking one of the store's cozys. Instead, you'll have your own that is far more comfortable and will reduce the heat on your fingers way more than typical cardboard cozys do.

Materials

For this project, you will need the following:

- A chunky yarn, one color.

- A crochet hook, size N.

- Your trusty scissors.

Instructions

Again, this is another incredibly easy project but, we will have to cover how to make a half double crochet stitch first. If you remember, the puff stitch is a variation of this stitch, so it will seem familiar at first. To make a half double crochet stitch, you would yarn over your crochet hook and insert it into a stitch. Yarn over your hook again, then pull the yarn through the stitch. If you've done this correctly, then you should have three loops on your hook. Yarn over your crochet hook again and pull the yarn through all three loops. This gives you the half double crochet stitch.

To make this drink cozy, start by making a chain of twenty stitches. Since we want this to be a round project, we will need to use a slip stitch, so, when you finish the last chain stitch, use a slip stitch to tie the ends together to create a round. This gives us the first row of the project. We want to move on to the next row, however, so we must next make a single stitch turning chain. From there, we will use half double crochet stitches in every link of the chain. This will give you a total of twenty half double crochet stitches in the second row. Again, we will use a slip stitch at the end to join the ends together and give ourselves a beautiful second row. Repeat this row until you have four rows of half double crochet stitches. You should have eighty half double crochet stitches by the end of the last row. To finish the project, we will use single crochet stitches for the final row. Doing so will serve to close up the bottom of the cozy and make it look like the chains on top.

And that's all there is to it. It's an easy project, but it'll get you practicing your half double crochet stitches, which is always a plus. These can also be used as armbands if you want. This is also a good method for beginning a sweater for your cat, though that kind of project will still take a bit more work to get right.

Project #5: An Infinity Scarf

This project is a lot harder than the last one, but boy does it ever look amazing. Infinity scarfs are amazing projects. You could play around with colors if you want, but we will be sticking to a single color for this tutorial. You'll soon find out that this doesn't decrease its beauty in any way, however. I suggest going with a light and soft color, nothing too vibrant. The scarf is an accessory after all and not the mean piece of an outfit.

Using a heavy yarn will help to keep the infinity scarf nice and warm during the winter, but the mixture of stitches we use will leave the scarf with lots of holes through which we can breathe. It will help to keep you warm but not stuffy, which is the best kind of wear for the winter.

Materials

For this project, you will need the following:

-   About three hundred yards of yarn, worsted or DK weight.

-   Crochet hook, size I.

-   A tapestry needle.

-   Your trusty scissors.

Instructions

Start your infinity scarf by first making the biggest chain you've ever seen. You will make a chain of 228 stitches. This chain will be huge, and it will also take you quite a while. You can definitely alter this pattern, too, so you can increase or decrease the number of stitches in your chain. A higher number will give you a larger scarf, whereas a lower one will give you a scarf that is a little smaller. Start here, then alter the pattern later once you are comfortable with it.

Use a slip stitch to connect the ends of the chain together. You will want to keep the chain as straight as possible during this step, as twists in the chain will lead to problems down the road. This step alone makes it the most complicated pattern we've looked at so far, but you've already known that since the second you started making the foundation chain.

Use a single stitch turning chain, and then use a single crochet stitch in each link around the chain. Since there were 228 links in the chain, that would mean that you're making 228 single crochet stitches. Yup—considering all the work that goes into making this scarf, maybe naming it "infinity" was a good choice after all. At the end of this never-ending row, add a three link turning chain. You'll remember that three links in a turning chain means that we're spacing it out for double crochet stitches. When we're working double crochet stitches like this, we would count the turning chain as the first stitch in the new row.

We've already used the first stitch of this row, next use a double crochet stitch in the next. Create a two stitch long chain, then skip the next two stitches and add a double crochet stitch into the third and fourth stitches. Continue the row by then skipping two stitches adding a double crochet stitch to the next two, skipping two stitches and adding a double crochet stitch to the next two. This pattern repeats until the end of the row where you will then slip stitch the ends together.

Before we jump into the next row, I want to take a moment to point out what we are doing. Some people may have caught on already why we use chain spaces between our double crochet stitches, but others might not have. We want to have an equal number of stitches in this row as the row below it, especially since we will be using a changing pattern throughout the rows, so we want to have a stitch we can push into at all times. Chain stitches in this row will help us secure our stitches in the following row, and it will also help to create a border that differentiates this row from the one above it.

Speaking of the row above it, make a single stitch turning chain, so you can get up to it. A single stitch turning chain can only mean one thing—we're using single crochet stitches on this level. Add a single crochet stitch into every single stitch from row two. This means you are adding one single crochet stitch to every chain stitch and double crochet stitch. Yup—that means you are doing another 228 stitches. This may be the kind of project you stretch out over the course of a week or two; ust don't forget to use a slip stitch to tie the end of this row to the beginning and make a three stitch turning chain.

This time around you may think that we're back to double crochet, but you're wrong. It's time to break out those half double crochet stitches you just learned in the last project. The turning chain still counts as the first stitch in this row though. Skip the second stitch, then, in the third stitch, you will begin this row's pattern. Add a half double crochet stitch to the third stitch, then make a chain stitch. Skip the next stitch and put another half double crochet stitch into the fifth stitch. Continue this pattern of half double crochet stitch, chain stitch, and skip a stitch until you get to the end of the row. Once you get to the end of the row, slip stitch the end to the second stitch in the row, thus being the first half double crochet stitch.

At this point, we will switch it up a little bit. The previous row or round should have ended with two chains next to each other. Use this space to slip stitch in and make a three stitch long chain that'll count as a stitch in the round. Use a half double crochet stitch in each chain stitch space. Follow each stitch up with a chain stitch, so it goes half double crochet stitch, chain stitch, until the end of the row, where you will then use slip stitching to connect the last piece to the second stitch. This time around, we will repeat this process for nine more rows. We don't need to worry about changing the formula because we're not counting the spaces by their numbers anymore, but by whether they are a chain or a half double crochet stitch. We put a half double crochet stitch into a spot where there is already one, so we know that we would use those stitches only with the chain stitches. We also know that we need to follow the half double crochet stitches with chain stitches, so, by the end, we always have the same amount of spaces filled with half double crochet stitches and with chain stitches, but each row alternates them slightly.

You've repeated that pattern nine times now, but on the tenth time, you will need to slip stitch yourself up to the next row and make a single stitch turning chain. Next, use single crochet stitches in each of the stitches, all 228 of them. Don't worry though, since you're almost done. End this round by slip stitching the ends of the round together, then making a three stitch long turning chain. The row that follows will be a repeat of the second row, way back from the early stages of the project. This means that you will double crochet into the second stitch. Now, you should fall into a pattern where you are creating two chain stitches, skipping two stitches, then double crocheting into the next two stitches. Again, this pattern looks like this: chain stitch, chain stitch, skip a stitch, skip a stitch, double crochet into the third stitch, double crochet into the fourth stitch.

You're almost done with the main part of the infinity scarf, but you need to finish by repeating the third row again. This is a single crochet row in which you add one single crochet stitch to each and every stitch in the previous row for a total of 228 single crochet stitches. By the time you're done with this project, you shouldn't have any problems with your single, double, or half double crochet stitches.

The rows are now done, but you will want to add some edging to your scarf to give it some great definition. There are many techniques you can use for this, especially those lacy techniques we looked at in the last chapter. However, in this case, we will stitch to a beautiful shell stitch. With a scarf of this size, we will be getting a total of 38 shells. We'll skip the first two stitches from where we are now, and then work the shell into the third stitch. Then, we'll skip the next two chain stitches and use slip stitching to start the next shell.

The shells themselves are a wonderful technique that you can use in many different patterns. For this type of stitch, you need to start with a double crochet stitch. Follow this with a single chain stitch and another double crochet stitch. Then, follow this again with another single chain stitch and a double crochet stitch. Repeat this two more times. You will have a pattern of double crochet, chain, double crochet, chain, double crochet, chain, double crochet, chain, double crochet. It's not very hard to do, but it is easy to lose count of how many stitches you've made for your shell. Remember that it starts with a double crochet stitch and alternates with chain stitches, and there are a total of five double crochet stitches and only four chain stitches.

Project #6: Leg Warmers

Alright, that last project was long and tough. If you aren't ready for another tough one, don't worry; I don't blame you. This time around, how about practicing your skills on an easier project that still uses a fair variety of stitches. These leg warmers are cozy, and they'll keep you warm during those colder days. Determining the length of the project will require you to first measure your legs or the legs that will be wearing the warmers. You will learn how to alter a crochet pattern to fit your own needs with this project.

Materials

For this project, you will need the following:

- Yarn, cotton, any color you want, medium weight.

- *[Recommended]* Two, three, or even four other colors of yarn to make your leg warmers stand out.

- A crochet hook, size J.

- A darning needle.

- A measuring tape.

- Your trusty scissors.

Instructions

We will be using a standard measurement when discussing this project. To keep everything that I am writing consistent, we will start with an 80 stitch long chain. I will continue to use this number in my discussion, but we will first talk about measurements and change up the pattern.

Since it is easiest to experiment on ourselves, let's take a measurement of our legs. Use your measuring tape to figure out how tall you want the warmers to be.

Typically, you will want to start just above the feet, or even, sometimes, you may want to cover half the foot with the warmer. This is up to you. Make sure you take down this measurement—you're going to use it to determine the number of stitches you will need. After you get this number, take a measurement around your leg that will be the length you want your foundational chain to be. You want to have a little bit of space beyond this, so add a little bit to your measurement, half an inch or a couple centimeters.

When you first start putting together your foundational chain, make ten chain stitches, and then pause. Pull out the measuring tape again and measure how long the chain is. Ten stitches is a good number because it is easy to divide your measurement by ten to get the size of each individual stitch, and, chances are, it'll take about ten until you can really see anything close to the size you'll need. Pay close attention to how long your foundational chain is and try your best to get as close to your target number as you possibly can. It is okay to go a little bit over or under, so long as it is close.

We're jumping ahead a little here, but you'll use your first measurement to determine how many rounds the warmers will have. More rounds equal longer leg warmers, so make sure that you alter this pattern to fit your own measurements; after all, that's the skill we're leveling up here.

Once you have your foundational chain of 80 stitches, move up to the second row and put a single crochet stitch into the first ten links in the chain. Next, you will create a chain stitch and turn the project around. Now, cover the rest of the row with half double crochet stitches for the next 70 links in the chain or so, until you reach the ten single crochet stitches you just made. Once you get to those last ten single crochet stitches, you will switch over to single crochet and double up on them. Once this is done, create a single stitch turning chain and turn your project over yet again.

This time, you will want to use single crochet stitches in the first ten stitches, but you need to be extremely careful to only use a single crochet stitch in the back loops of these ten stitches. Once you have done that though, you will then half double crochet stitch into the back loops of the rest until you reach those ten single crochet stitches at the end. You'll then use single crochet stitches again, and, once again, you'll make sure only to use the back loops of these lap ten stitches.

As you may have expected, we will be making a single stitch turning chain next, and moving back up in a similar fashion. This means we'll start with ten single crochet stitches, and then switch over to half double crochet stitches in the middle. At the end of the row, we'll switch back over to single crochet stitches again. Remember to always turn your project over once you switch rows. Also, at this point, remember that we're sticking with the back loops. We can repeat this pattern over and over and *over and over* again endlessly— however, instead, why don't we measure the size of the project and determine how many more rows we will need to reach our desired size.

Once you get to the size that you are looking for, you will use your trusty scissors to cut the yarn, leaving about a foot long tail, which you will then tuck away, as per usual. You could use slip stitching to bring the leggings together, but it will be easier to use your darning needle to tie the edges together. Once you do, you will then have a single leg warmer. You'll want to keep track of how many stitches you used during each step of the project.

Because that's only the first one. You still have the second leg to work with, meaning you will also require two warmers. Have fun!

Project #7: A Pillow

This final project isn't as hard as the infinity scarf that we made, but it still has challenges of its own. We will be making a pillow that is soft as can be, so we have a place to comfortably lay our heads down after we finish with our projects. This time around, we will learn two more steps that we haven't covered yet. The first is that we're going to play with stuffing; a pillow needs stuffing to be squishy, after all. The other technique we'll practice is creating a heart to serve as the centerpiece of our pillows.

Materials

For this project, you will need the following:

- Yarn, bulky weight, color A.

- Yarn, bulky weight, color B.

- A crochet hook, size K.

- A crochet hook, size H.

- A tapestry needle.

- Stitch markers.

- Polyester filling.

- Your trusty scissors.

Instructions

We'll start this with the pillow itself and then create our heart separately to be added to the project. So, to begin, start with a foundational chain of four stitches. Use a slip stitch to attach the fourth chain to the first chain and create yourself a round.

For the first round, or row, we will start by creating a chain of three stitches. Starting from the center of your loop, you will start with two double crochet stitches, then a treble crochet stitch. This is followed by three double crochet stitches and a treble crochet stitch in the next link in the chain. Add three double crochet stitches and one treble crochet stitch to the remaining stitches. This should give you one chain with two double crochet and one treble crochet stitch, and three links in the chain with three double crochet and one treble crochet stitch. When you finish the last link in the chain, use a slip stitch to attach it to the top of the three stitch chain from the start of the round.

Create another three chain stitches to serve as a turning chain. Next, work a double crochet stitch into the first two stitches. From there, you will get the stitch that represents the corner; use two double crochet stitches, a treble crochet stitch and two more double crochet stitches. This will set up the pattern for this round. The next three stitches will have a double crochet, but then the fourth—the corner—will have two double crochet stitches, a treble crochet stitch, and two more double crochet stitches. Use a slip stitch at the end of the round to attach it to the third stitch in your turning chain, just like you did previously.

The next three rounds will follow the same pattern. Start the round with a three stitch turning chain, then double crochet into each of the stitches except the corners. The corner stitches will require you to work two double crochet stitches, a treble crochet stitch, and two more double crochet stitches. When you get to the end of the round, use a slip stitch to attach the end to the third link in the turning chain. As you follow this pattern for these three rounds, you will find that your pattern keeps getting larger. This is normal—there should always be sixteen more stitches in this round compared to the one before it.

At this point, we have been working exclusively with our first color: color A. Now that we're reaching the sixth round, it's time to switch to color B. Start by creating a single stitch turning chain, single crocheting into each of the stitches in the previous row except for the corners. When you get to the corners, you will be working four single crochet stitches into them. At the end of the round, you'll use a slip stitch to attach the end to the beginning, this time attaching the end to the single stitch turning chain.

We would create another single stitch turning chain, and, this time, we will work a single crochet stitch into the turning chain. With this first single crochet stitch out of the way, we can then turn our attention over to our repeating pattern; this time around, it is a treble crochet stitch followed by a single crochet stitch. Alternate between treble crochet and single crochet stitches in all the stitches this round, except for the four corner stitches where you'll work four single crochet stitches into place. A slip stitch joins the end of this round to the starting turning chain. We finish this round by creating another single stitch turning chain, then single crocheting into every stitch except the four corner stitches that receive the four single crochet stitches.

We will be repeating these two rounds three times each for a total of six rounds. So, this starts with a single stitch turning chain, a single crochet into the turning chain, and then alternating treble crochet stitches and single crochet stitches in all the stitches except for the corners, which will receive four single crochet stitches. The end of the round is slip stitched shut, and a single stitch turning chain is made. Single crochet stitches are added into every stitch except for the corner stitches, which get four single crochet stitches each. If you count the first two rounds in which you discovered this pattern, then your pillow will have a total of eight rounds that follow this pattern.

That's the end of the first step of your pillow, though this only gives you one half of the pillow. Before you finish, you will still need to go through and create another fifteen rounds, following these instructions. This will give you the backside of the pillow. Use your tapestry needle to attach three of the four sides of the front and back together. You can then stuff the pillow full of polyester to give it a soft and comfortable feel, and then sew it shut when you are finished.

We want to stick a heart into the middle of the pillow though. As it is right now, we just have a small square in the middle of the pillow that stands out from the rest. We will place our heart right in the center of the pillow. You may want to create two hearts—one for each side, to keep it looking even.

Creating a crochet heart starts with a magic circle and, from there, moves out. Create a three link chain, then work in three treble crochet stitches, three double crochet stitches, a single stitch chain, a treble crochet stitch, a single stitch chain, three double crochet stitches, three treble crochet stitches, and a three stitch long chain. This is then slip stitched to the center of the circle. The second round begins with a three stitch long turning chain. Single crochet and half double crochet into the first stitch of the round, then add three half double crochet stitches into the next stitch. The third stitch gets two half double crochet stitches, but the next four stitches will receive a single crochet stitch each. Create a single stitch chain, then double crochet into the next. Chain one again, then single crochet in the next four stitches, followed by two half double crochet stitches in the one after and three half double crochet stitches in the following. The last stitch of the round gets a half double crochet and a single crochet stitch before you would make a three stitch long chain and slip stitch the round to the center of the heart.

The third and final round in your heart starts with a three stitch long turning chain. Begin the round proper by working two single crochet stitches into the first stitch. The second stitch will receive three half double crochet stitches while the third stitch only receives two half double crochet stitches. The next nine stitches then get only a single crochet stitch. The tenth stitch is also a single crochet, but it is followed by a single stitch chain, then a single crochet stitch in the next nine stitches. Follow this with two single crochet stitches in the next stitch, a single crochet stitch in the following, and two single crochet stitches in the last. Create a three stitch long chain and use a slip stitch to attach it all together, and you have yourself a heart.

Now, simply attach your heart, make sure it is secure, fill your pillow up with stuffing, and sew the last side shut. And there you have it—a brand new pillow to lay your head down on.

Next Chapter

In the next chapter, we will discuss a few of the more common mistakes that beginners tend to run into when first starting with crochet. Use this as a guide for what not to do.

CHAPTER SIX

MISTAKES TO AVOID

Hopefully, you've continued to read ahead to this point before running off to do the projects in the last chapter. If you did, then congratulations. By reading this chapter first, you just made your life a lot easier. It's fun jumping into the projects, but it can be incredibly frustrating. There's a ton of mistakes that you can make along the way that can slow down your progress and really make the experience a bummer of a time.

Keep in mind that these mistakes can still be useful. When we realize that we've made a mistake, and we take it upon ourselves to go back and figure out what we did wrong, we get better at problem solving and even better at crochet. This applies to any skill you are trying to learn. However, there is still an emotional component to making a mistake, which could make us feel negatively after realizing we've made it. Beginners make tons of mistakes, although it is important to realize that that is what beginning is. Accept that you *will* be making these mistakes, and learn from them. Heck, you'll probably even make some of the mistakes in this chapter, even after you've become aware of them. That is how mistakes for you—they just happen.

On the other hand, this chapter can still give you a heads up. I hope it helps you to avoid some of the more common mistakes, but, if it doesn't, then, hopefully, it will still help you identify them quicker.

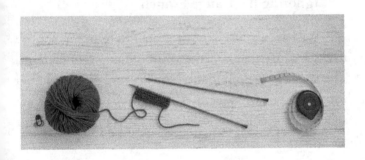

Understanding the Differences Between Crochet and Knitting

Crochet and knitting both work with fabrics to create textiles. They both use long, slender objects to join fabrics together. The movements for crochet and knitting are quite different from one another, if you know anything about the two skills; however, if you don't, then they may as well be identical. This makes it no surprise that people often confuse these two art forms together.

Hopefully, you didn't pick up this book thinking it was about knitting. If you did, then sorry! But, if you've stuck around for this long, then I hope you'll still enjoy this relaxing new skill! The big difference is that knitting uses two needles to work the yarn, whereas crochet uses a crochet hook.

Ignoring the Gauge Swatch

We haven't talked much about this term yet, but you may see gauge mentioned throughout different patterns. The gauge is the number of stitches and rows fit into a four by four inch square. This is a way of seeing what size the project is supposed to be. This is important for two reasons.

We will skip the first reason because it is the next mistake we're going to look at. That just leaves us with the second, which is all about the tension in your work. As you work through a project, you will come to find the amount of tension you need the product to have to keep its size, which can be incredibly difficult to get right when you are first starting out. So, before you jump into a new pattern, look to see if it lists a gauge. You can make a gauge swatch. If you mess it up, no worries—just try again. You will only lose the time and yarn it takes to make a small swatch, but it can save you lots of time and disappointment down the road.

Using Yarn of the Wrong Weight

This is the other element for why you want to get the gauge of swatch made to begin with. If you use a yarn that is too light, then you will find that it takes more rows to make a swatch. If that happens, then you will want to increase the weight of your yarn. If your yarn is too heavy, then it will have an adverse effect, and you will find that it takes fewer rows to finish the swatch. Decrease the weight to fix it.

If you know that you will be using a yarn of a different size, then you may want to take a look at the next mistake.

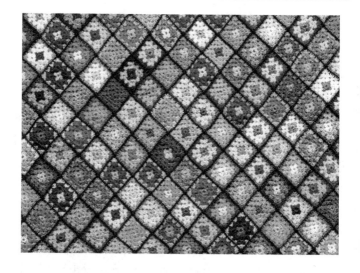

Don't Be Afraid to Alter a Pattern

This one is going to take you a little bit to gain confidence in doing, but, if you've done the projects in this book, you'll be equipped for it. If you have a heavy yarn, and you want to do a project that needs a lighter yarn, don't just give up. You can still use the heavy yarn for the project, but you will need to be creative about it. You can't just follow everything the pattern says.

Instead, you will want to take measurements for yourself. Create your gauge swatch according to the pattern and see how much bigger or smaller it is. You will need to do a bit of simple math. If it takes fewer rows to fill it out, then you know you need to use less yarn overall. You'll need to use your measuring tape and be mindful of the stitches you make. This work is best done with some practice rounds to get it right.

However, you absolutely can do it, and, if you want to go from being a beginner to a more practiced apprentice, then this is something you absolutely have to learn.

Your Sides Change Sizes

When you're putting together a project, you want your rows or rounds to stay the same size. It's a pretty good idea since nearly every project uses uniform rows when you're a beginner. However, beginners also tend to have a real problem with their rows changing sizes. The rows either get bigger or smaller as they move from one row to the next. What gives?

This is a simple problem with a simple solution. What is happening is that you are stitching into a different stitch when you change rounds. You are either supposed to stitch into the second or third but are going one earlier, or you are supposed to stitch into the first but going into the second. If you find yourself stuck making this mistake, then you need to practice getting your chains right.

Chapter Summary

- Mistakes are good things. They can be frustrating, but they are also chances to learn. You shouldn't try to avoid making mistakes; instead, you should try to limit them.

- Despite how we opened the book with it, it is important to point out again that crochet and knitting are not the same thing.

- Many patterns come with a gauge swatch. This is a four by four inch square made up of the design, so you can ensure you are using the right materials.

- It is important to use yarn of the right weight when following a pattern exactly.

- Don't be afraid to alter a pattern. Being able to take a pattern and change it as you need to is one of the most important skills you can focus on training once you get your stitches down.

- Be careful to always stitch in the right chain. Many beginners tend to stitch too soon or late and get a project that shrinks or grows between rows.

FINAL WORDS

So, there you have it. When you entered this book, I assumed you were coming from a place of zero to limited knowledge about crochet. This entire book was based on taking you from a starting place of zero knowledge and giving you the metaphorical tools you need to start your journey toward crochet mastery.

Of course, that journey will take you some time—like a really, *really* long time. We only started out by learning about crochet in chapter one. In chapter two, we discovered the tools used to crochet. Chapter three was where the meat of the knowledge was, and it's all about those essential crochet stitches that make up the majority of the projects you'll be encountering over the next few years.

In chapter four, we continued with more general techniques, though we'll talk more about chapter four in just a moment. Chapter five is, of course, filled with projects for you to practice and learn with. These projects each focus on teaching you different elements of the skill, so I hope you'll try them all. Chapter six was the final chapter, and this just covered some of the mistakes that beginners make. Now you're here!

So, let's talk about chapter four. In this chapter, we looked at a brief overview of about 30 different styles of crochet. There is a ton of stuff that you can use in that chapter to decide what you want to learn next. You don't need to go grab another book or sign up for a course to figure out how to improve your skills; just pick a style that sounds cool and interesting to you and start learning the necessary stitches and tricks to make your own awesome projects.

That's all there is to it.

So, I hope you go out there and start making all sorts of amazing creations!

CPSIA information can be obtained
at www.ICGtesting.com
Printed in the USA
LVHW100847071120
671027LV00064B/2446